Uniforms of the German Colonial Troops • 1884-1918

Uniforms of the German Colonial Troops
1884-1918

• Schutztruppen • Polizeitruppen • Kaiserliche Marine • Kaiserliche Marine-Infanterie • Ostasiatische Expedition Korps •

Charles Woolley

Schiffer Military History
Atglen, PA

Acknowledgement

The author expresses his sincere thanks to Peter Harrington, Curator of the magnificent Anne S.K. Brown Military Collection, Brown University, Providence, RI. Peter's cheerful help and willing assistance in finding little known references in the Collection makes the job of preparing volumes like this a great deal easier, as well as richer.

My thanks and love to patient Nancy who once more made it work. My deepest appreciation and gratitude to Bob Biondi who continues to let me wander the minefields of obscure and undocumented military subjects not yet covered.

Book design by Robert Biondi.

Library of Congress Catalog Number: 2009932085.

Printed in China.
ISBN: 978-0-7643-3357-6

We are always looking for people to write books on new and related subjects. If you have an idea for a book, please contact us at the address below.

Published by Schiffer Publishing Ltd.
4880 Lower Valley Road
Atglen, PA 19310
Phone: (610) 593-1777
FAX: (610) 593-2002
E-mail: Info@schifferbooks.com.
Visit our web site at: www.schifferbooks.com
Please write for a free catalog.
This book may be purchased from the publisher.
Please include $5.00 postage.
Try your bookstore first.

In Europe, Schiffer books are distributed by:
Bushwood Books
6 Marksbury Ave.
Kew Gardens, Surrey TW9 4JF
England
Phone: 44 (0)20 8392-8585
FAX: 44 (0)20 8392-9876
E-mail: info@bushwoodbooks.co.uk
www.bushwoodbooks.co.uk

Contents

Introduction: A Short-Lived Empire

The first half of the 19th century witnessed slow development of German overseas commerce and the necessary shipping capacity to develop sea trade required to create overseas colonies. By the 1860s, ocean shipping capabilities were on the increase through the creation and subsequent business activity growth of companies such as the North American Lloyd Lines and the Hamburg-America Lines.

Four important trading companies operating in overseas regions that were later to become colonies, were O'Swald on the East Coast of Africa, Woermann in the Kameruns and Deutsch-Südwestafrika, and in the Pacific, Godeffroy, and Hernsheim and Company operating in the copra trade.

In the 1840s and 1850s many German political writers promoted "colonial consciousness" in an effort to stem the problem of German emigration to America and to foster overseas expansion. "The North German Confederation" in its expansion into the new German Empire furthered the notion of the need to add colonial possessions. At first Bismarck, in power at the time, was opposed to the acquisition of colonies, believing that all emphasis should be centered on building a strong Germany at home. With increasing pressure from Germans then trading abroad who were facing a need for protection, as well as pressure from the two powerful societies formed in the early 1880s, the "Kolonialverein" and the "Gesellschaft für deutsche Kolonisation", Bismarck relented and agreed to support their requests for protection for their overseas activities. The "Kolonialverein", the Colonial Society founded in 1882 with over 10,000 members in three years, and the "Gesellschaft für deutsche Kolonisation", the Society for German Colonization, joined their forces to form the powerful and formidable "Deutsche Kolonialgesellschaft", the German Colonial Society. In April 1884, Bismarck, after pressure from these sources, placed under Imperial protection the "establishments" of the powerful German merchant Lüderitz in Deutsch-Südwestafrika. This move was quickly followed by the founding of the larger colonial empire in Africa, as well as islands and territories in the Pacific. In six years the Empire, at its height, covered a land area of a million square miles, with a native population of fifteen million.

This was a rather extraordinary increase in the six years from 1884 to 1890, after which there were fewer acquisitions made. The trading companies, not the government in Germany, negotiated with the native tribal leaders, for minimal value, many of boundaries of the African colonies. This later led to bitter disputes between the German colonists and the natives that in turn necessitated protection forces financed by the Motherland. The Schutztruppe, the protection force, coupled with a Polizeitruppe, smaller in size, was created to bring these disputes under control, by force if necessary.

The German Empire, at its height in Africa, consisted of Togoland, the Kameruns, Deutsch-Südwestafrika, and Deutsch-Ostafrika. Holdings in the Pacific were the West and East Caroline Islands, Yap, Admiralty, Bismarck Archipelago, Kaiser Wilhelm's Land which was part of New Guinea, New Pomerania, one of the Soloman Islands, the Marshall Islands, the two islands of German Samoa, Savoli Upou, and on mainland China, Kiautschou (the German spelling of Kiao-Chow) with its important enormous Naval base of Tsingtau located on the edge of the Yellow Sea.

The African colonies were protected in large by the Schutztruppe, while in the Pacific islands the job was left to small groups of native police. In China, the Marine III. See-Bataillon protected the area around the Naval base at Tsingtau, and the Ostasiatischen Expedition Korps was ready for any needed action in the Pacific.

World War I ended Germany's dreams of empire. The Tsingtau Chinese holdings quickly fell to Japan in 1914. Soon after Togo and the Kameruns fell to the French, and Deutsch-Südwestafrika fell to Botha's mixed forces. Under the leadership of Colonel Letow-Vorbeck, Deutsch-Ostafrika held off Allied force attacks until the end of hostilities in November 1918. Today these former German African colonies are named Republic of Cameroon (Kamerun), Togolese Republic (Togo), Barundi, Rwanda, Tanganyika (Deutsch-Ostafrika), and Namibia (Deutsch-Südwestafrika).

What follows are descriptions and illustrations of the unique uniforms and equipment of German and native troops in the African colonies. Included in separate sections are the uniforms of the *Marine III. See-Bataillon* and the *Ostasiatischen Expedition Korps*.

CHAPTER ONE

Schutztruppen Uniforms - the Home Service Pattern

Schutztruppen uniforms of the Home Service pattern, plus a few field accessories, are shown in the following illustrations. Published sources used are *Militär Information-Tafeln* by Kunstmaler Carl Henckel, Pirma, b. Dresden 1900; *Militär-Informations-Postkarten*, Militär Kunst Verlag, Pirma, b. Dresden, painted by Carl Henckel, 1899; two editions of *Die Deutschen Schutztruppen in Afrika*, Moritz Ruhl, Leipzig; *Uniformen der Marine und Schutztruppen*, Zigarettenfabrik, Waldorf Astoria; postcards produced by the "Kolonialkriegerdank", Berlin, 35 Potsdamer Str. 98a, and *Uniformenkunde Das Deutsches Heer* by Knötel, Pietsch, and Collas. second edition, W. Spemann, Stuttgart, 1982.

As evidenced by these drawings, the only uniform distinction between colonies was the color of the facings: red for Togo and the Kameruns, white for Deutsch-Ostafrica, and blue for Deutsch-Südwestafrika.

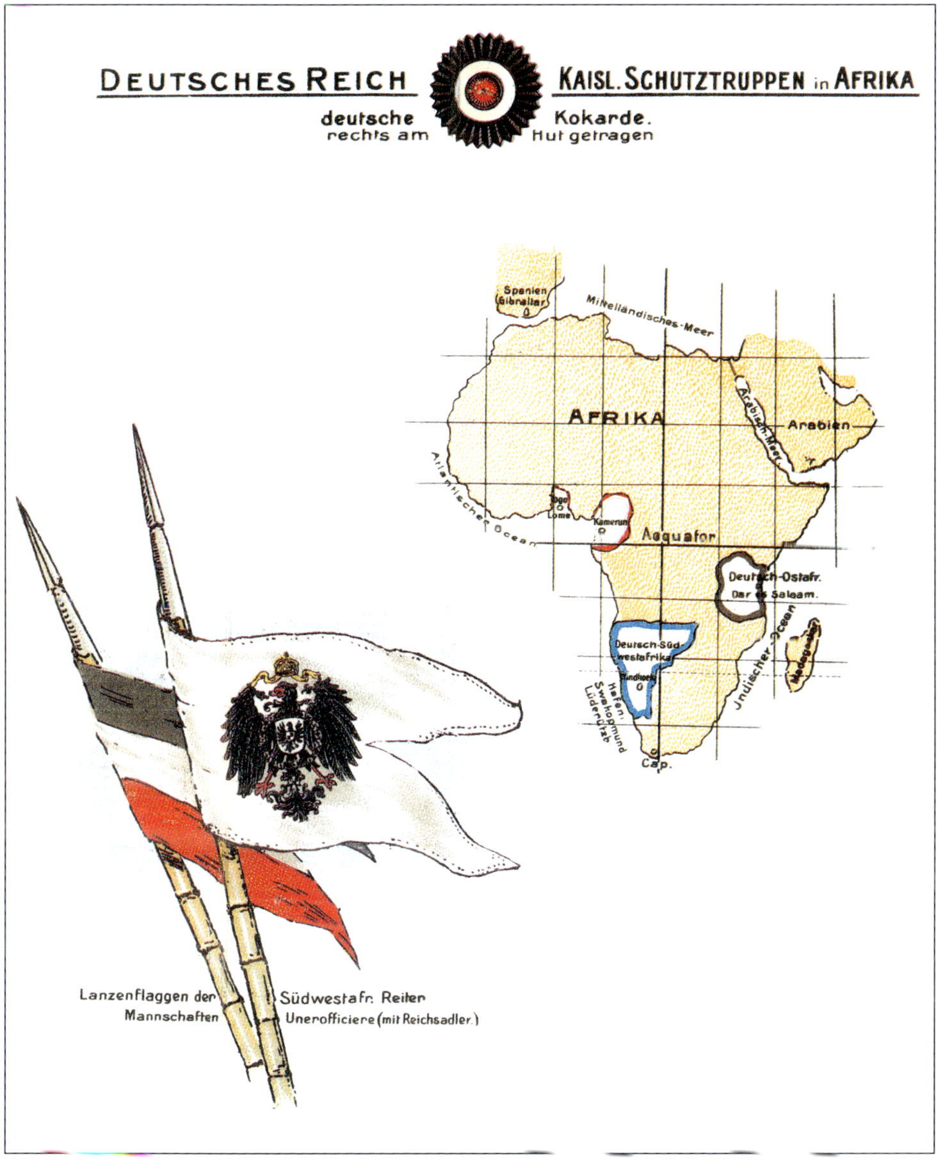

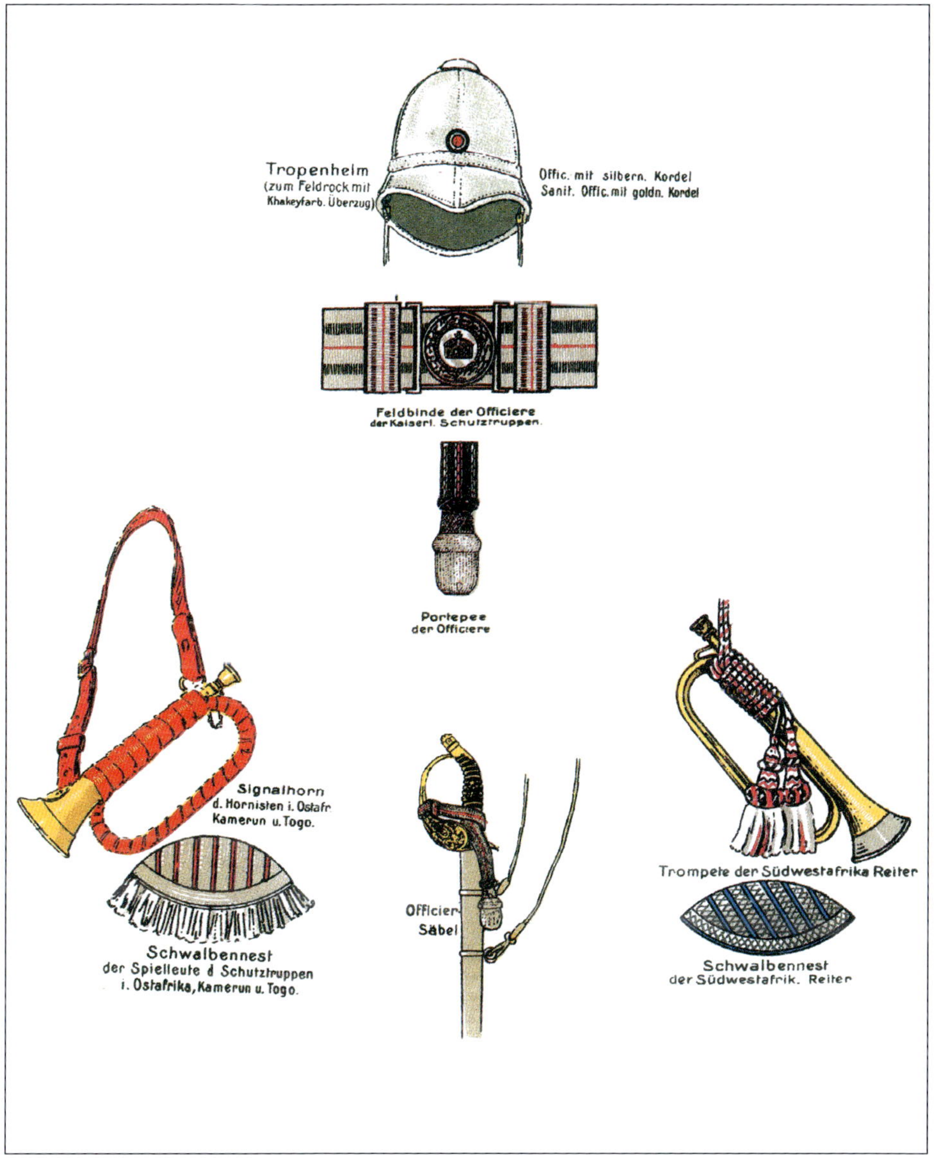

Upper: Map of Africa showing the locations of the German colonies prior to World War I. Militär Information-Tafeln. Kunstmaler Carl Henckel, Pirma.

Lower: Lance pennons for the South West Mounted Troops. Carried by enlisted men on the left and by NCOs on the right.

Center: Tropenhelm, Dress Belt for Officers, Portepee for Officers; Colonial Officer's Sword; Left: Signal Horn for Deutsch-Ostafrica, Kamerun, and Togo, with the Schwalbennest Shoulder Device for musicians in the same areas; Right: Trumpet and Schwalbennest for mounted troops in Deutsch-Südwestafrika. Militär Information-Tafeln. Kunstmaler Carl Henckel, Pirma.

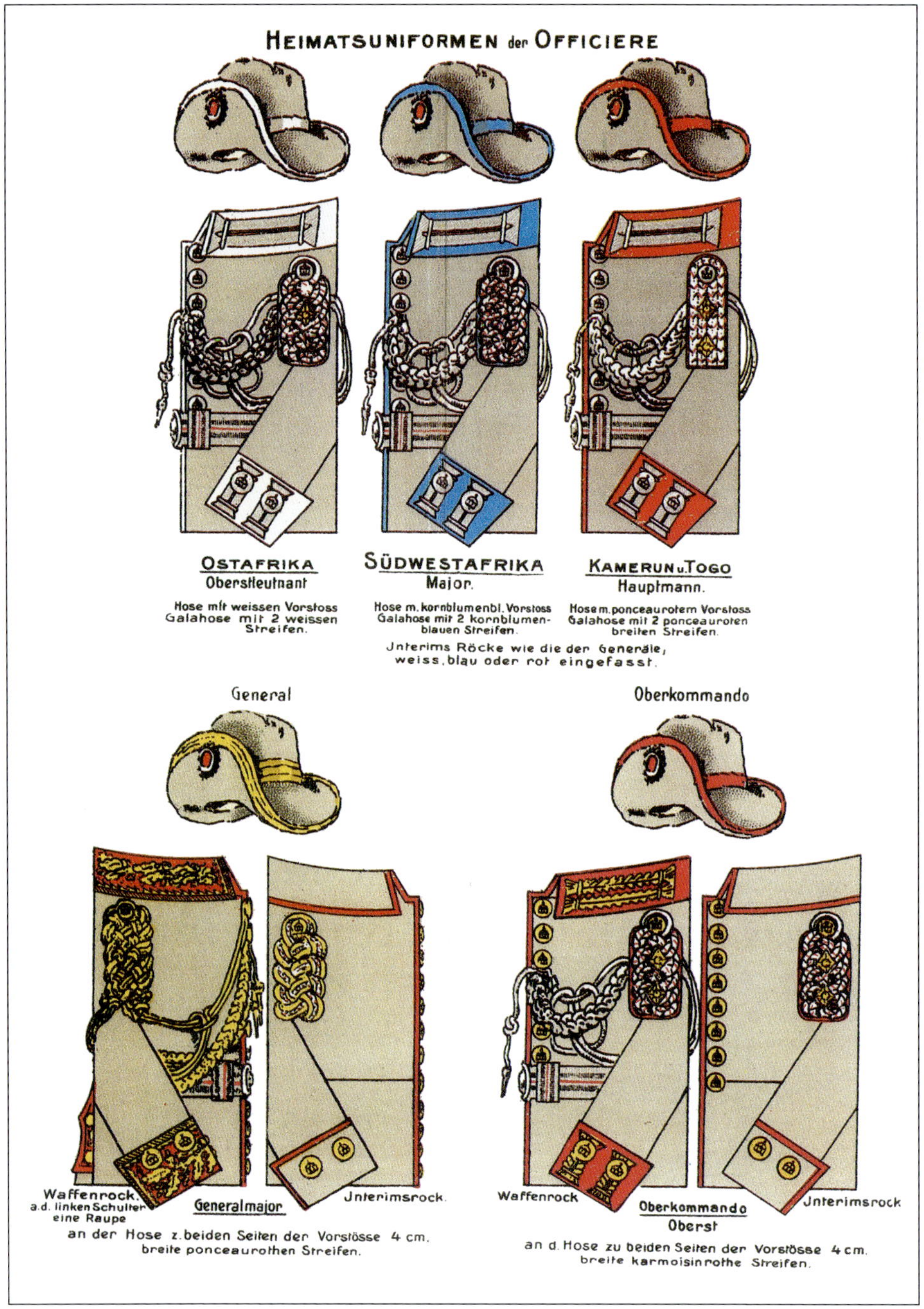

Home Service uniforms: Generals, Colonels, and lower ranking officers, with distinctive color piping for the three colonies. Militär Information-Tafeln. Kunstmaler Carl Henckel, Pirma.

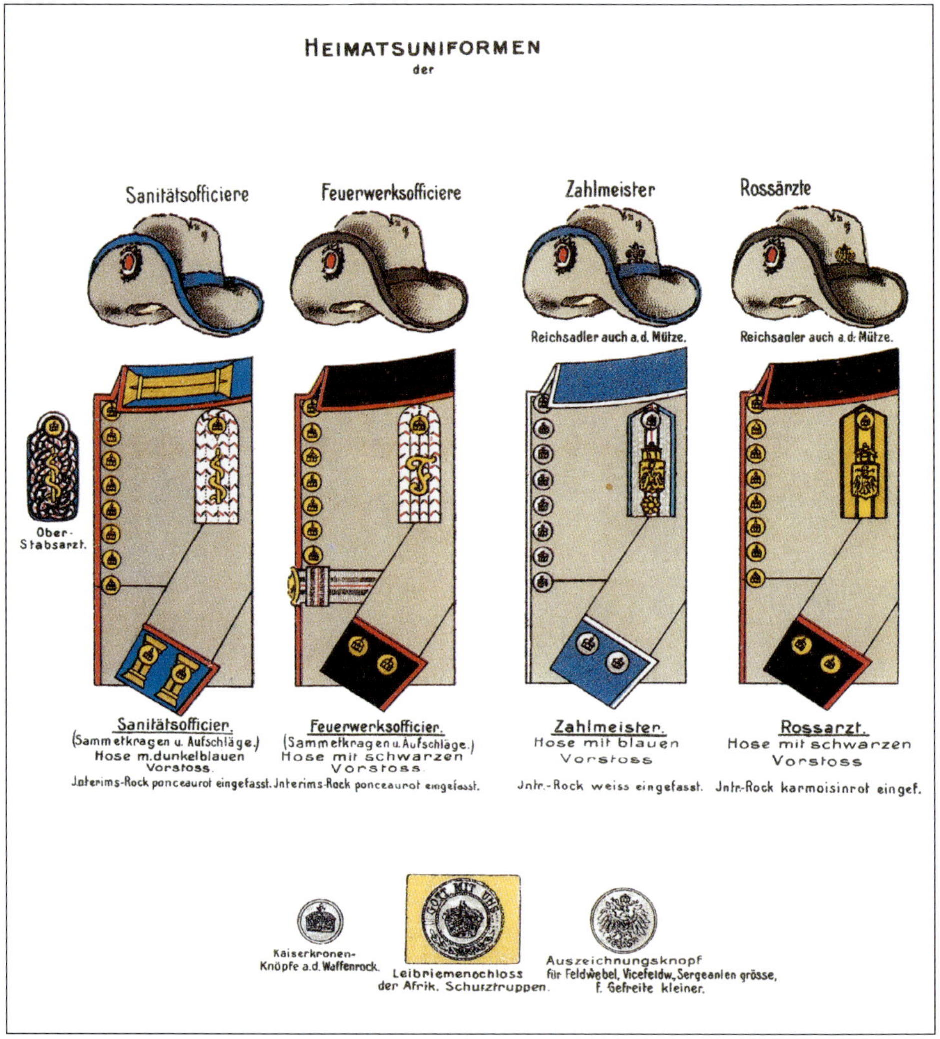

Home Service uniforms for officers of the various branches of service. Militär Information-Tafeln. Kunstmaler Carl Henckel, Pirma.

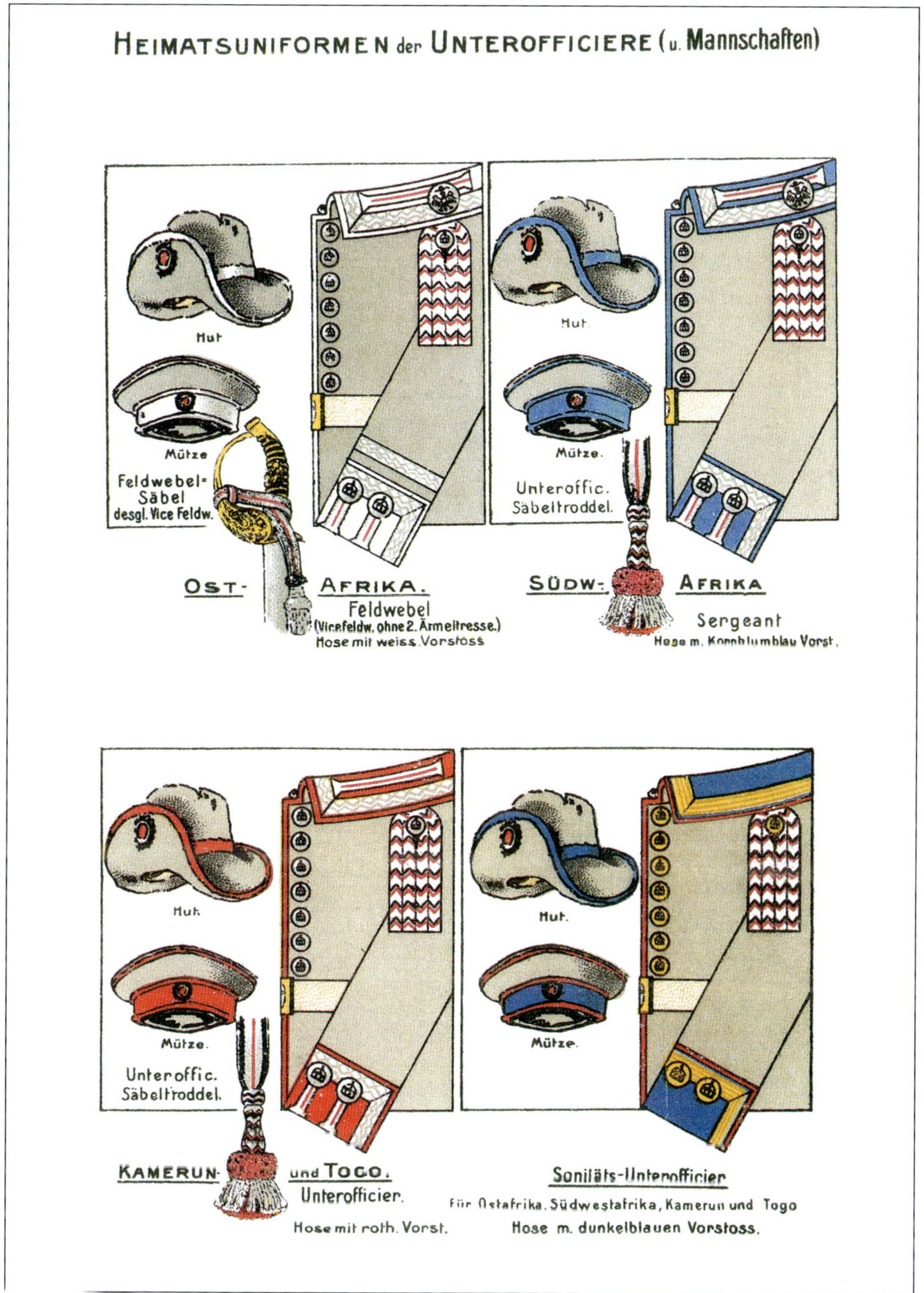

Home Service uniforms for Unterofficiere (NCOs) by colony, with an additional illustration of hospital services.

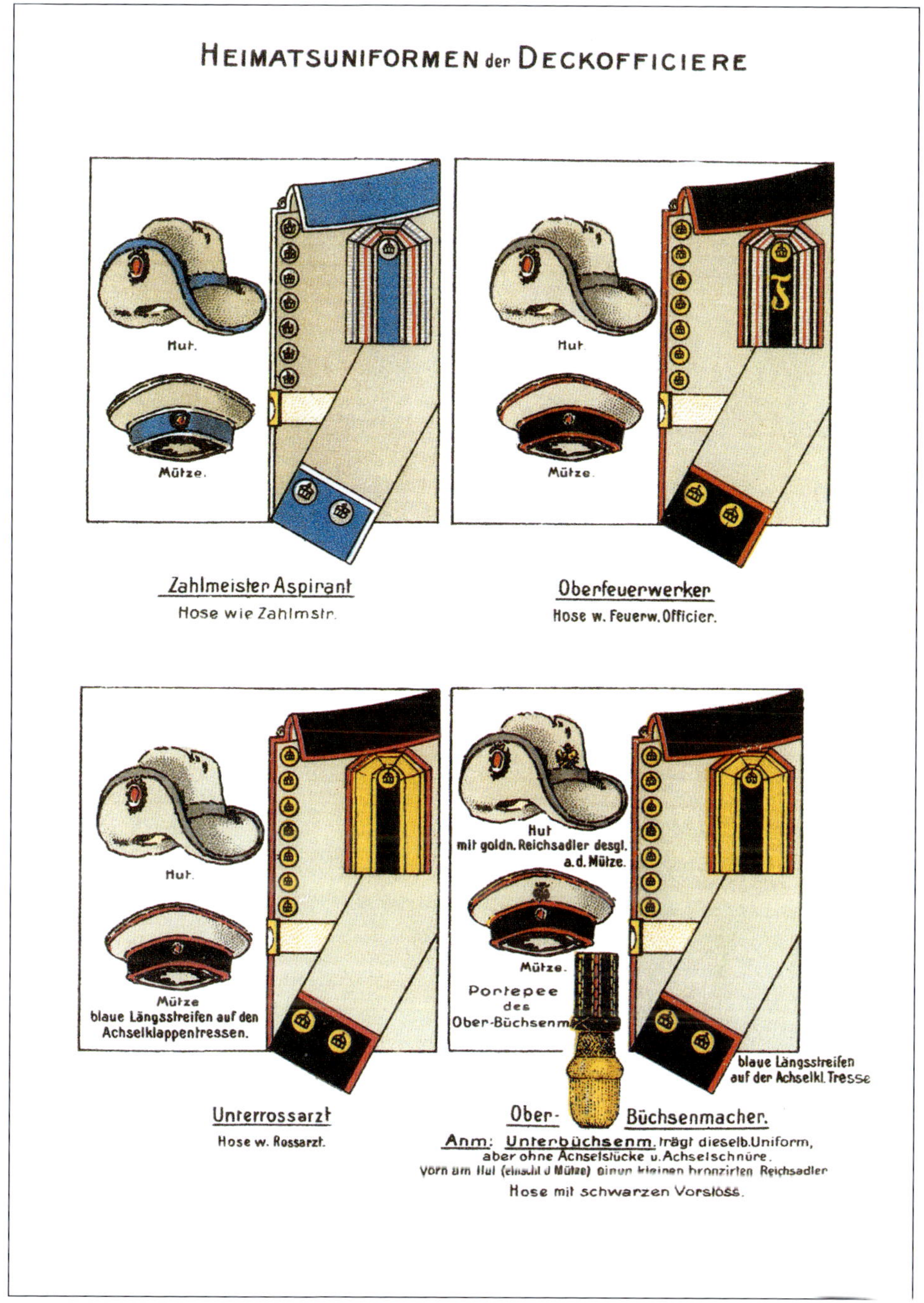

Home Service uniforms for Warrant Officers, Pay, Ordnance, Medical, and Weapons. Militär Information-Tafeln. Kunstmaler Carl Henckel, Pirma.

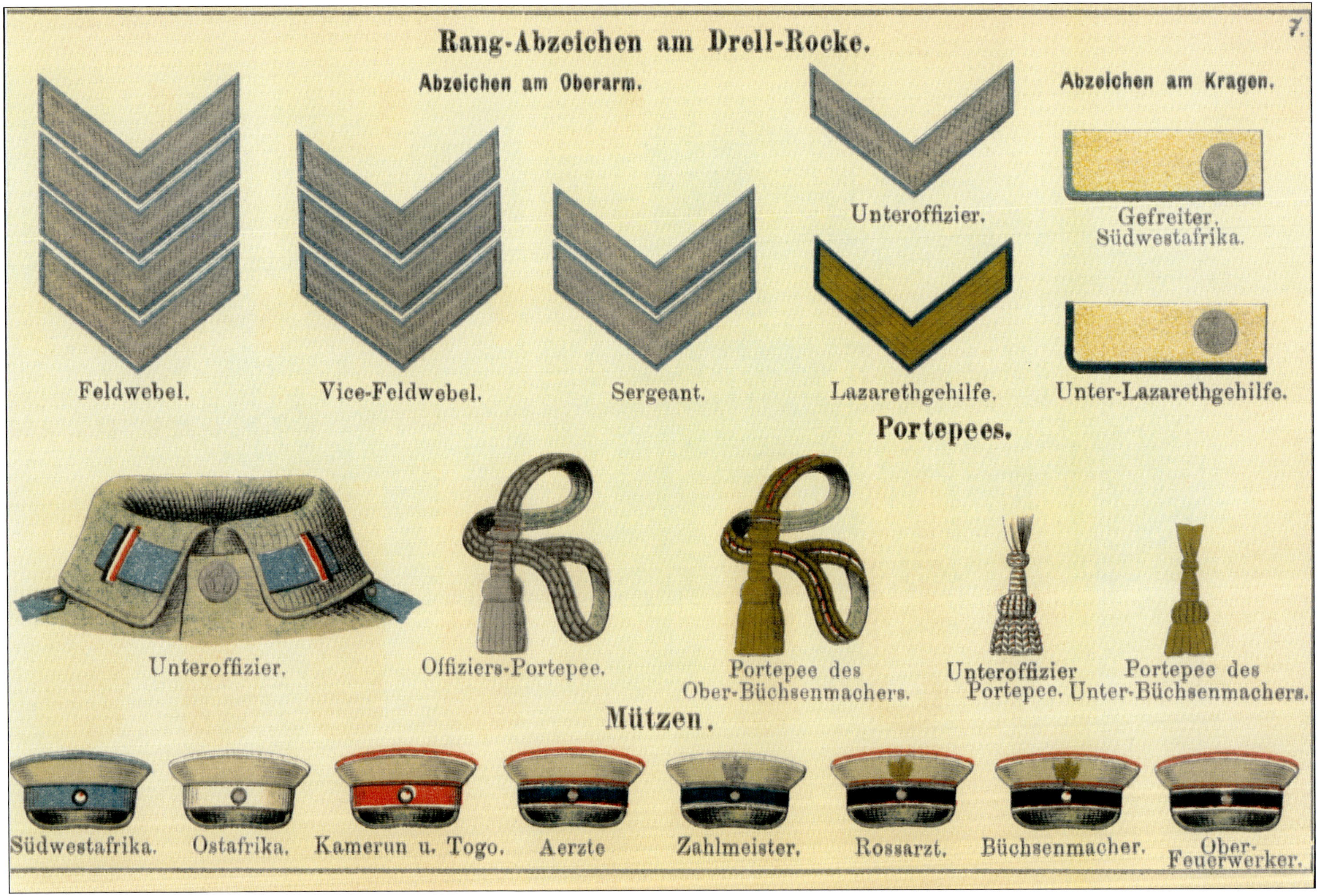

Schutztruppe NCO rank insignia, portepees and caps. Die Deutschen Schutztruppen in Afrika, Moritz Ruhl, Leipzig.

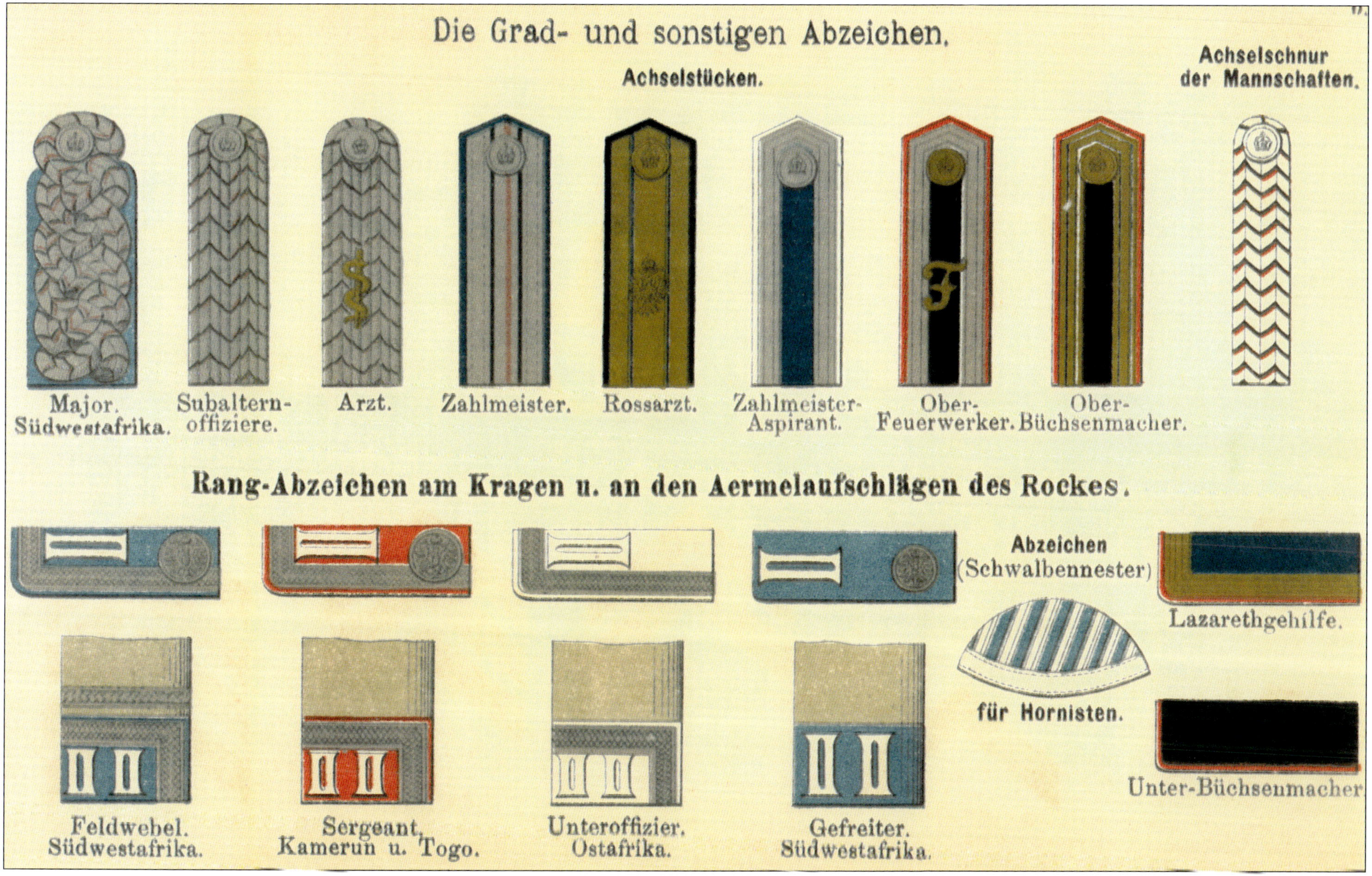

Schutztruppe officer and NCO rank insignia, Die Deutschen Schutztruppen in Afrika, Moritz Ruhl, Leipzig.

Militär-Informations-Postkarten No.15 Kaiserliche Schutz-Truppen für Afrika. Sergeant Kamerun, Unteroffizier Süd West-Afrika, Feldwebel Ost-Afrika. Schematic of the variations of Home Service uniform insignia.

Two patriotic colonial postcards. The card depicting three figures is by Willy Stöwer who is more recognized for his fine marine paintings.

Colonial administration officer. Uniformen der Marine und Schutztruppen. Waldorf Astoria.

Colonial administration officer on Home Service. Uniformen der Marine und Schutztruppen. Waldorf Astoria.

Studio portrait of Generalmajor von Deimling in Schutztruppe full dress and decorations.

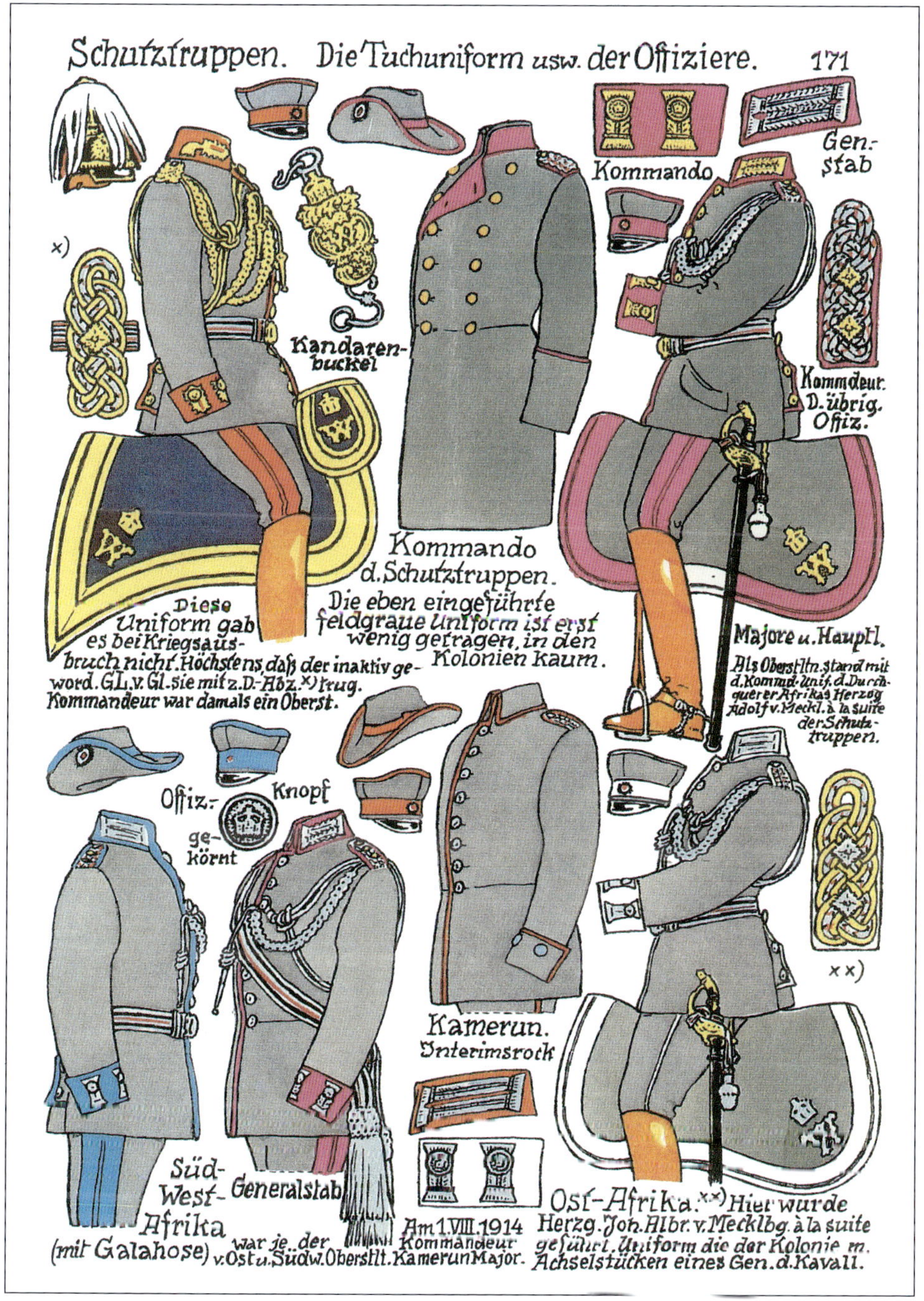

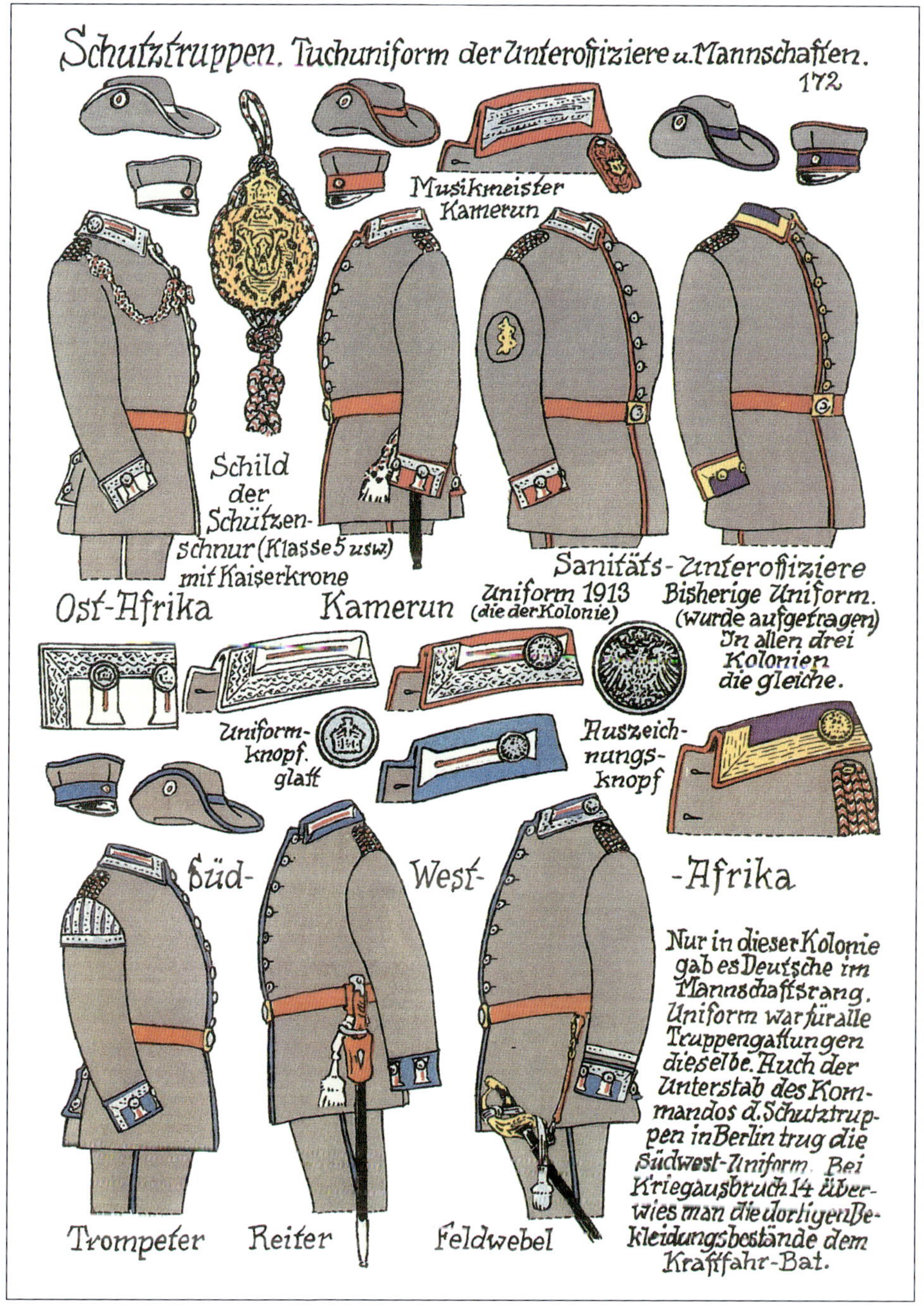

Pages 17-18: Paul Pietsch, with his profound interest in Imperial Colonial uniforms and equipment, painted the following four illustrations for the second 1982 edition of Uniformenkunde Das Deutsche Heer originally by Herbert Knötel. Pietsch teamed up with Major A. D. Baron Collas in adding greatly to Knötel's original work. The German captions are self-explanatory.

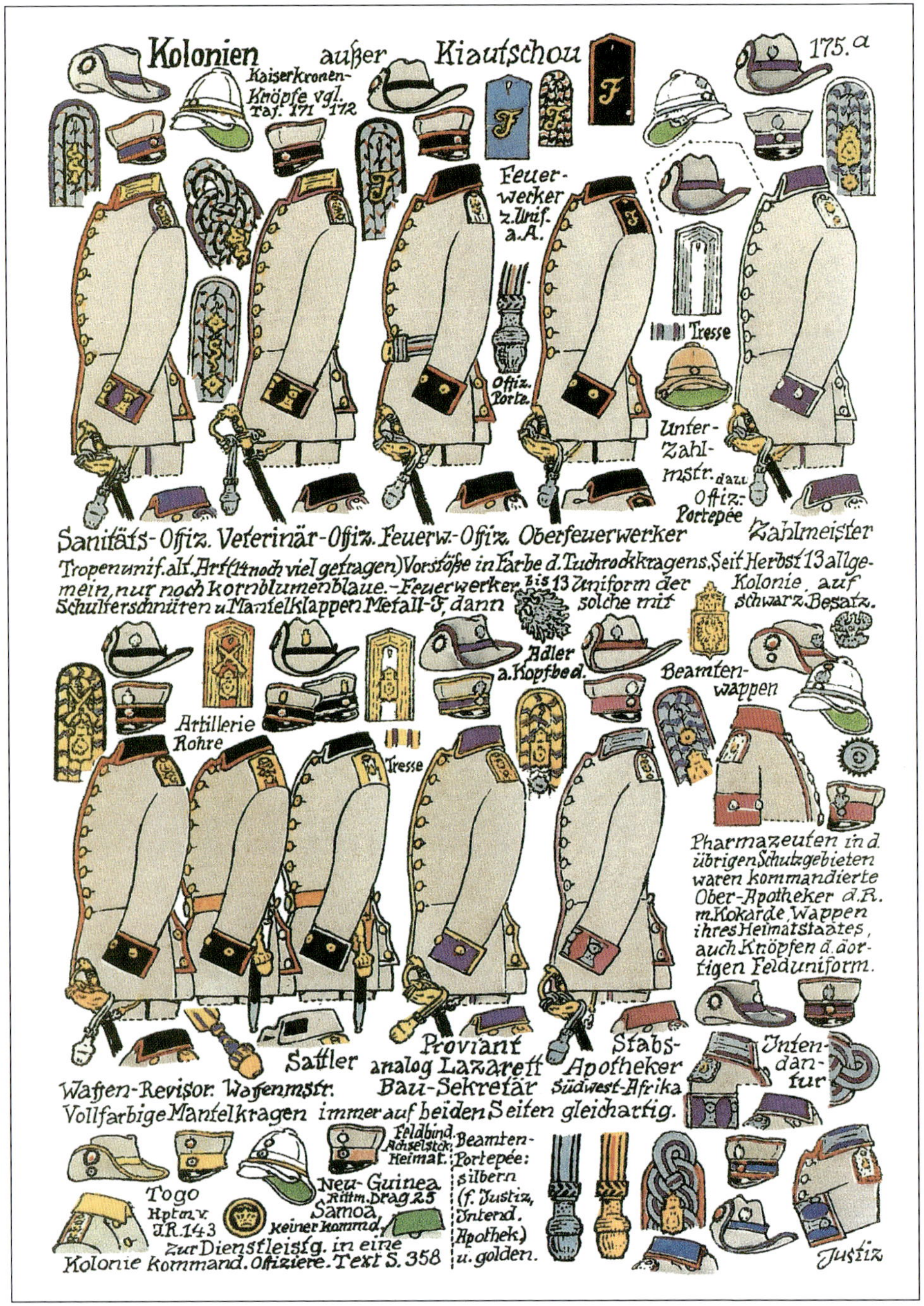
Kolonien außer Kiautschou 175.a
Kaiserkronen-Knöpfe vgl. Taf. 171 172
Feuerwerker z.Unif. a.A.
Tresse
Offiz. Portep.
Unter-Zahlmstr. dazu Offiz.-Portepée
Sanitäts-Offiz. Veterinär-Offiz. Feuerw.-Offiz. Oberfeuerwerker Zahlmeister
Artillerie Rohre
Adler a.Kopfbed.
Beamtenwappen
Tresse
Waffen-Revisor. Waffenmstr. Sattler Proviant analog Lazarett Bau-Sekretär Stabs-Apotheker Südwest-Afrika Intendantur
Togo Hptm.v. J.R.143
Neu-Guinea Rittm. Drag.25 Samoa
Justiz

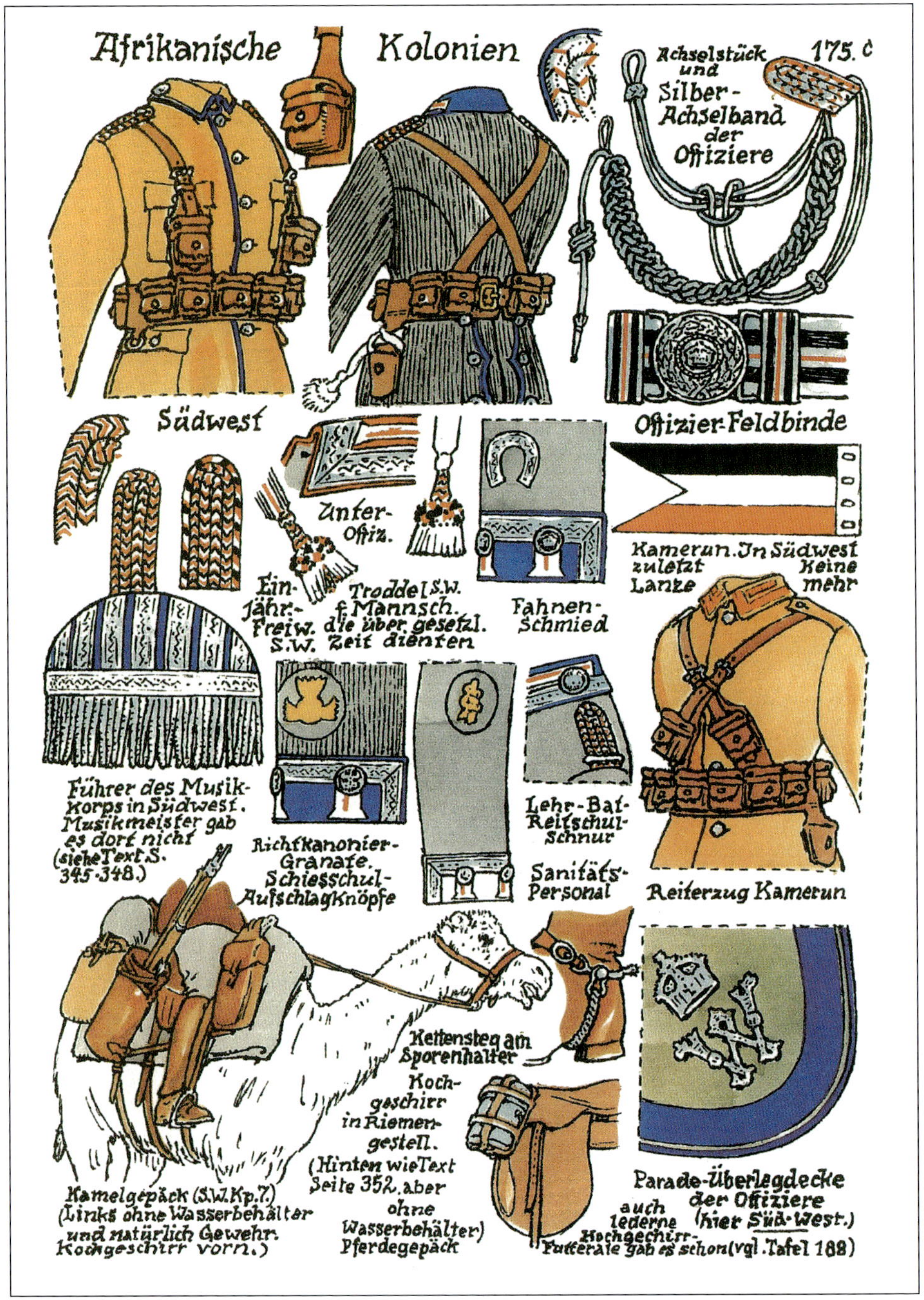
Afrikanische Kolonien 175.c
Achselstück und Silber-Achselband der Offiziere
Südwest
Offizier-Feldbinde
Unter-Offiz.
Einjähr.-Freiw. S.W.
Troddel S.W. f. Mannsch.
Fahnen-Schmied
Kamerun. In Südwest zuletzt keine Lanze mehr
Führer des Musikkorps in Südwest.
Richtkanonier-Granate. Schiesschul-Aufschlagknöpfe
Lehr-Bat. Reitschul-Schnur
Sanitäts-Personal
Reiterzug Kamerun
Kettensteg am Sporenhalter
Kochgeschirr in Riemengestell.
Kamelgepäck (S.W.Kp.7.)
Pferdegepäck
Parade-Überlegdecke der Offiziere (hier Süd-West.)

CHAPTER TWO

Kamerun (Cameroon) and Togo

In 1889 the original Kamerun and Togo Schutztruppen, or protective troops, were formed and consisted of:

- One Hauptmann, or Captain, as Commander of the Schutztruppe in Kamerun
- One Premierleutnant as Commander of Schutztruppe in Togo. The two colonies were jointly administered at this time
- Two Leutnants
- One Doctor, or Medical Officer
- Nineteen Unteroffiziere, or NCOs
- One Hospital Assistant
- One Paymaster
- One Armament, or Ordinance, as well as Signal Officer
- Three Hundred Native Troops

In 1914 this force had grown to 61 officers, 17 medical personnel, 23 civilian personnel with military rank, 98 NCOs, and 1,550 native troops.

The Kamerun Schutztruppe uniform for the native soldiers was made of khaki material and was identical to that worn by the native soldiers of the Ostafrika Schutztruppe, with the exception that the collar was red and bore Garde Litzen in yellow of the type worn by officers and NCOs on the Home Service uniform.

The native troops wore a short, or low-crowned red fez. Pinned to the fez was a small silver-plated colonial-style eagle. The fez was also decorated with a black tassel of woven silk or wool. The trousers were made of the same khaki material, knee length, worn with sand grey leggings and brown ankle boots, although, often, no boots were worn. All other equipment was of brown leather identical to that worn by the other colonies. Rank insignia was also the same as that used in the other colonies, while native NCOs were permitted to wear the wide-brimmed bush hat piped in red.

Togo, officially founded 2 July 1884, because of its limited size was afforded a Polizeitruppen rather than a Schutztruppen. Reichskanzler Bismarck approved the formation of a Polizeitruppe on 30 October 1885. This force originally consisted of ten members, which by 1894 after several reorganizations, grew to one white and six native NCOs, six native Gefreiters and 144 native enlisted men.

In 1896 the Reichstag authorized the formation of a Schutztruppe in Togo. The Colonial governor felt there was no need for a Schutztruppe, and did not follow the authorization as the Polizeitruppe had things well in hand.

The earliest uniforms of the Polizeitruppe consisted of white Naval dress with red facings and piping. Illustrations by Carl Henckel dated 1899 show a Togo native unteroffizier in a uniform which appears Naval in cut, but made of khaki drill, with no leggings or boots. In the 1890s the native uniform consisted of a khaki tunic with a low-cut standing collar of red material and with red piping and shoulder straps. The trousers were knee length, the red fez was retained, and a red sash completed the uniform. Equipment included the M71 rifle, Pionier Faschinenmesser, canteen, breadbag, mess gear, and ammunition pouches as issued to regular German troops. Between 1908-1913 the last uniform changes were made. German officers and NCOs took the final Colonial pattern with red piping on the Home Service uniform and on the hat band. Red collar and cuffs were worn on the field service uniform. For the enlisted Polizeimanschaften, the uniform remained the same; only the red fez was ultimately replaced by the all khaki visor cap. The Togo German officers and NCOs wore a white tropical summer uniform when the occasion arose.

Early in World War I, on August 24, 1914, Togo sued the French and British governments for peace. The surrendering force consisted of 198 Germans, 5 active and 9 reserve officers, 600 local police, and four machine guns. The French and British force consisted of 2,000 active soldiers, 10,000 native mounted lancers, seven field cannon, and seven machine guns; not good odds for the Germans.

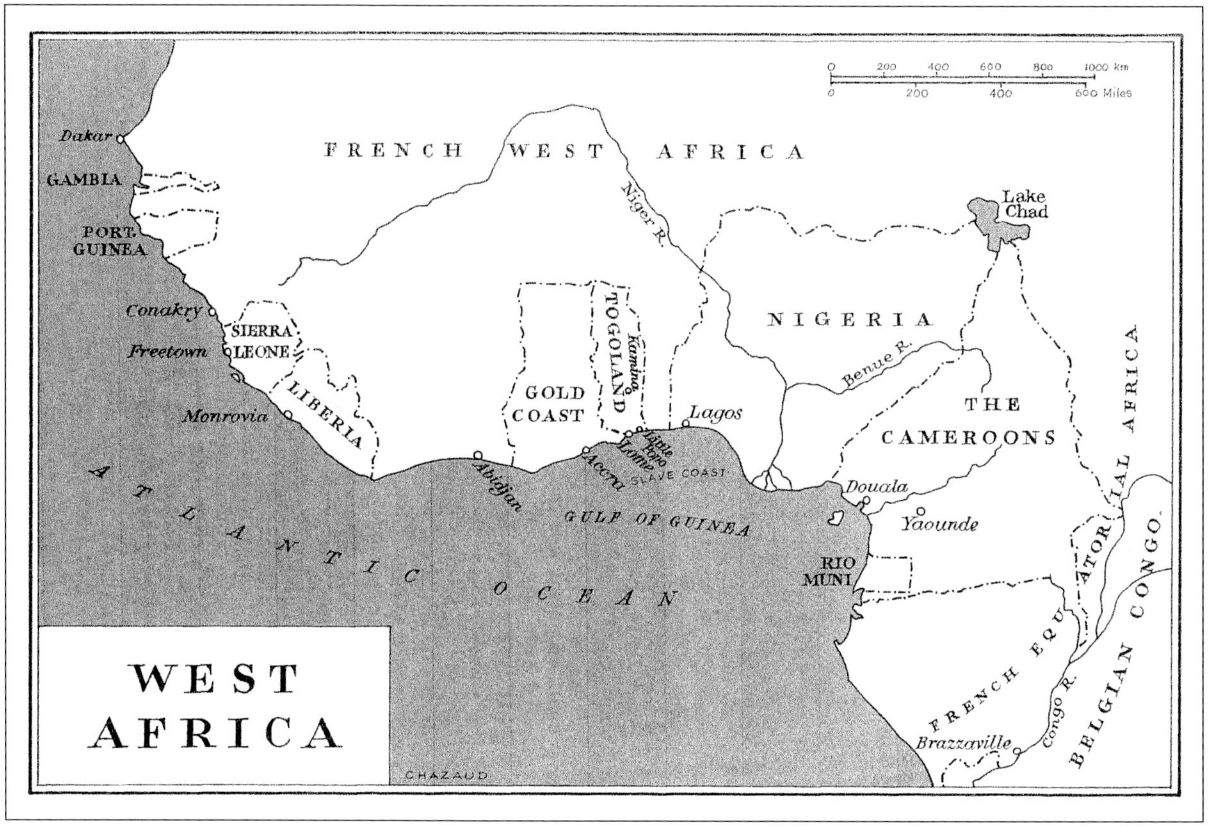

Map of West Africa showing the location of Togo and Kamerun.

A Ruhl illustration titled Schutztruppe für Kamerun und Togo clearly shows the red piping of those two colonies on the sand grey "Dienst" uniforms and the cornflower blue retained on the summer white and khaki-colored uniforms

Ruhl's oversized or poster size uniform plate titled Schutztruppe für Kamerun und Togo illustrates L/R Unter-Buchsmacher Home Service, Zahlmeister Aspirant Home Service, Offizier Home Service, Offizier Parade Home Service, Sanitäts-Unteroffizier Tropical Field Uniform Khaki Drill, Unteroffizier Tropical White Uniform.

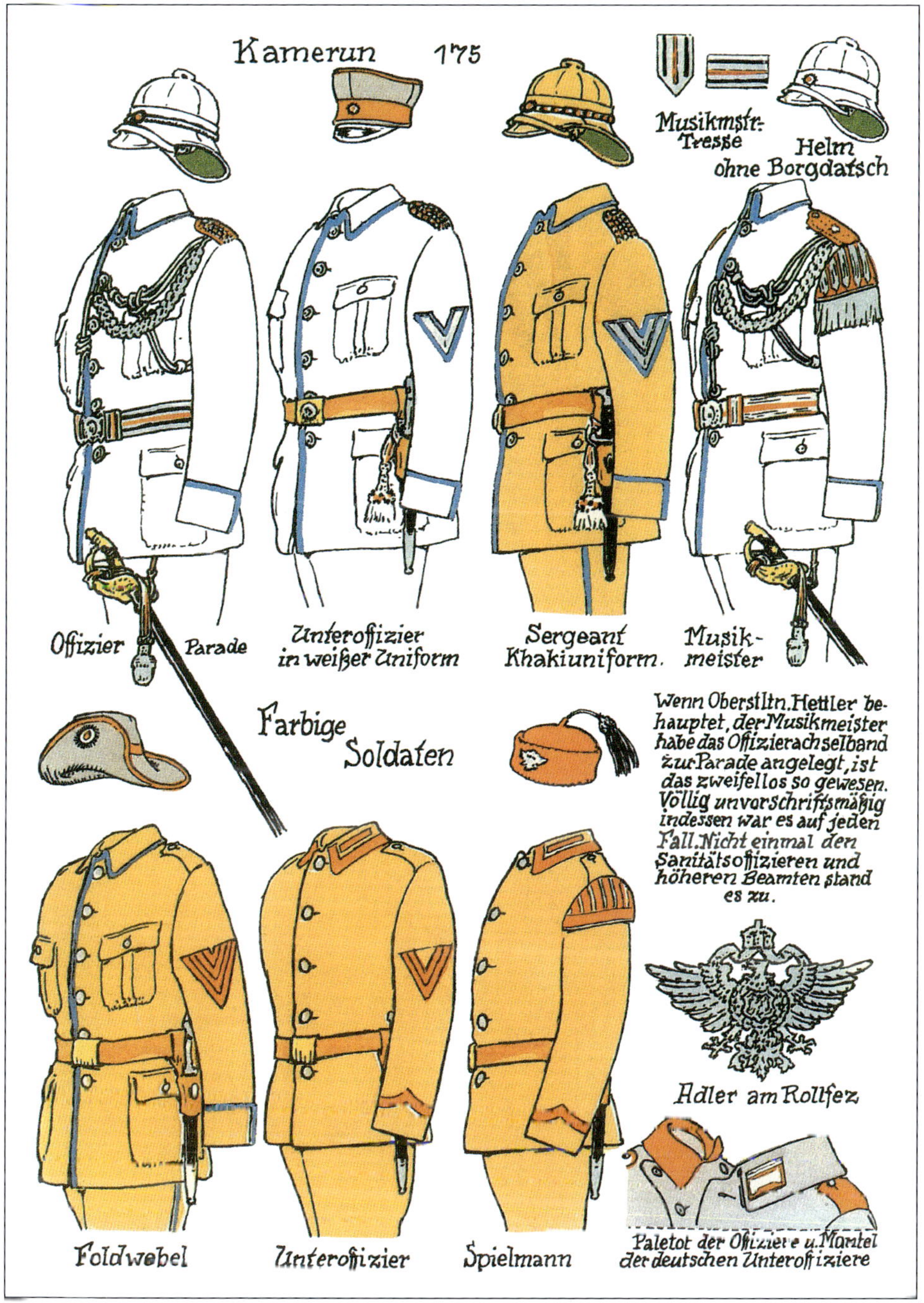

Paul Pietsch's uniform illustration for Kamerun. The lower three figures depict native troops. Uniformenen Das Deutsches Heer.

Paul Pietsch illustrates a native Unteroffizier and a Feldwebel for Major Eberhard Hettler's Marineinfanterie und Schutztruppen. The Unteroffizier wears a post-1900 tunic, but retains the red fez as seen in the prior illustration. Shoes or boots do not seem to be standard issue for the lower ranks. The Feldwebel is dressed in the same uniform as his European counterpart.

Carl Henckel's Militär-Informations-Postkarten No.18 portrays a medical officer, the station-chief, and a Feldwebel all in summer tropical white uniforms, two pictured with the tropenhelm. All Europeans wear uniforms, white and khaki, piped in cornflower blue, although the Unteroffizier shows the Togo and Kamerun red trim on his wide-brimmed hat. The Askari Unteroffizier is dressed in the native uniform in fashion prior to 1900. His red fez, rather than the later style Tarbusch, is tassled and carries a small colonial-style eagle. Note the sailor-type blouse styling of his tunic, the red sash, red chevrons and trim to the blouse which is not in cornflower blue. The Unteroffizier is armed with a Kar.88 and a M 86 revolver.

Leutnant, Interimrock of the Home Service Uniform. Uniformen der Marine und Schutztruppen. Waldorf Astoria.

Schutztruppe Kamerun, Captain, White Tropical Summer Uniform. Uniformen der Marine und Schutztruppen. Waldorf Astoria.

Kamerun Sergeant in khaki field uniform. Post duty. Uniformen der Marine und Schutztruppen. Waldorf Astoria.

Askari enlisted man in khaki field uniform complete with red fez. Uniformen der Marine und Schutztruppen. Waldorf Astoria.

Native Schutztruppe Feldwebel drilling the troops. Uniformen der Marine und Schutztruppen. Waldorf Astoria.

Native NCO musician. Uniformen der Marine und Schutztruppen. Waldorf Astoria.

Commanding Officer Police Troop, Togo. Tropical uniform. Uniformen der Marine und Schutztruppen. Waldorf Astoria.

Police Troop, Kamerun. Enlisted man on custom duty. Uniformen der Marine und Schutztruppen. Waldorf Astoria.

Polizeimeister, Police Troop, Kamerun. White tropical uniform. Uniformen der Marine und Schutztruppen. Waldorf Astoria.

Police Troop, Togo. Enlisted man in field marching order. Uniformen der Marine und Schutztruppen. Waldorf Astoria.

Mounted native Unteroffizier, Kamerun. His uniform consists of a red fez with a black tassel, khaki tunic with a red collar trimmed with yellow braid, red braid on the edge of the cuff and rank chevrons, also in red. The NCO is barefoot and carries a lance with a red, black, and white pennon. R.J. Marrion. Tradition magazine.

CHAPTER THREE

Deutsche-Ostafrika (German East Africa)

The development of Deutsch-Ostafrika (German East Africa) began in the early 1880s when a group of German merchants joined together to create the "Deutsch Ostafrikanisches Gesellschaft" described as a "Colonial Society." The sale of ivory was their first order of business, followed closely by trading in spices, primarily cloves.

Kaiser Wilhelm II, upon his ascension to the crown, was given by his grandmother, Britain's Queen Victoria, the territory surrounding Mount Kilimanjaro, including the mountain itself, adding to the size of the colony. Germany had hoped to slow down the migration of its people to the United States and Australia, and this region with its cool highland climate attracted German farmers in significant numbers. Wildlife abounded and was well known for its quantity and variety. Natural protection for the colony came on its western flank from an inhospitable region, which was malarial ridden and densely foliated.

In the late 1890s the Colonial Office and the Reichstag yielded to pressure from the colonists and their administration to substantially build up the strength of the Schutztruppen. Recruiting from regular units at home and a massive incorporation of native troops called Askaris swelled the ranks. The native troops were superb pathfinders and scouts, with the additional assets of physical hardiness and immunity to tropical diseases so destructive to Europeans.

Throughout World War I, the Askari number never exceeded 4,000, but they quickly became the leading fighting force in Africa. The Askari were led by competent and well-trained German volunteer officers and NCOs who soon became fluent in speaking the native Swahili language and, as importantly, adding to their acceptance, were dedicated to the well being of their troops. Morale was high and the commander, Colonel, later Lt.Gen. Paul Von Lettow-Vorbeck, was a great leader and communicator while addressing and training the native troops in their own language. Lettow-Vorbeck's success fighting the Allies with his Askaris from 1914 to 1918 is legendary and fills many books with its details. This success tied up in Africa thousands of Allied troops sorely needed on the western front, which was Lettow-Vorbeck's basic plan.

The Askaris were originally equipped with the Gew.M71 of Mauser design, 11mm, single shot firing black powder which, because of its smoke, made concealment difficult in battle conditions. Supplies of Kar.88s and later Gew.98s slowly replaced some of the Gew.M71s, and after 1914, captured British SMLE Mark IIIs were issued firing .303 smokeless cartridges. Machine guns were the Maxim MG 01, and later updated to the MG 08. The 7.5cm Gebirgskanone L/17 of 1908 and the 10cm Kanone 04 made up the weapons of the field artillery units.

The uniforms for the Askaris were cotton khaki material with shoulder straps and a stand and fall collar. The trousers were of the same material and were generally worn with blue grey legwraps and brown ankle boots. The headgear completing the uniform was a khaki tarbusch, or fez-style cap, with a protective neck flap to shield the shoulders and neck from the intense tropical sun. A small silver colonial eagle was attached to the front of the tarbusch for the mannschaften, with a larger version of the same eagle for unteroffizier wear. Askari troops, on occasion, decorated the crown of their tarbusch with long green leaves or tufts of grass as seen in illustrations to follow. Rank insignia was worn on the sleeve, as was the company number on the early pattern uniforms. The rank insignia for senior and junior NCOs was made of a red flat braid and was worn in the standard Army pattern. Early pattern buttons were in brass, later replaced by silver, embossed with the Imperial crown. Specialty qualification patches were worn above the NCO stripes, or singly on enlisted tunics.

The Home Service uniforms for the European Schutztruppen of Deutsch-Ostafrika were the same as those worn by those in Deutsch-Südwestafrika with the exception of the Waffen Farbe, or branch color, which was white. A change of the white Waffen Farbe was made to the khaki tropen, or tropical field uniform and the white cotton summer dress uniform, both of which were piped in the Südwest cornflower blue. In Deutsch-Ostafrika widespread use of the tropenhelm, or tropical helmet, was evidenced. The cork body was covered in white or khaki cloth with a colonial eagle in gold gilt for officers, with a gilt spike with a perlring mounted on a quatrefoil base. For garrison use the tropenhelm had a white covering material, while in the field the material was khaki. Spikes were not worn on these helmets, but were replaced by a ventilating button. The helmets for Deutsch-Südwestafrika had silver fittings rather than the gold gilt.

In 1914, at the outbreak of World War I, the strength of the Schutztruppe in Deutsch-Ostafrika was reported at under 3,000, with the majority being Askari, or native troops.

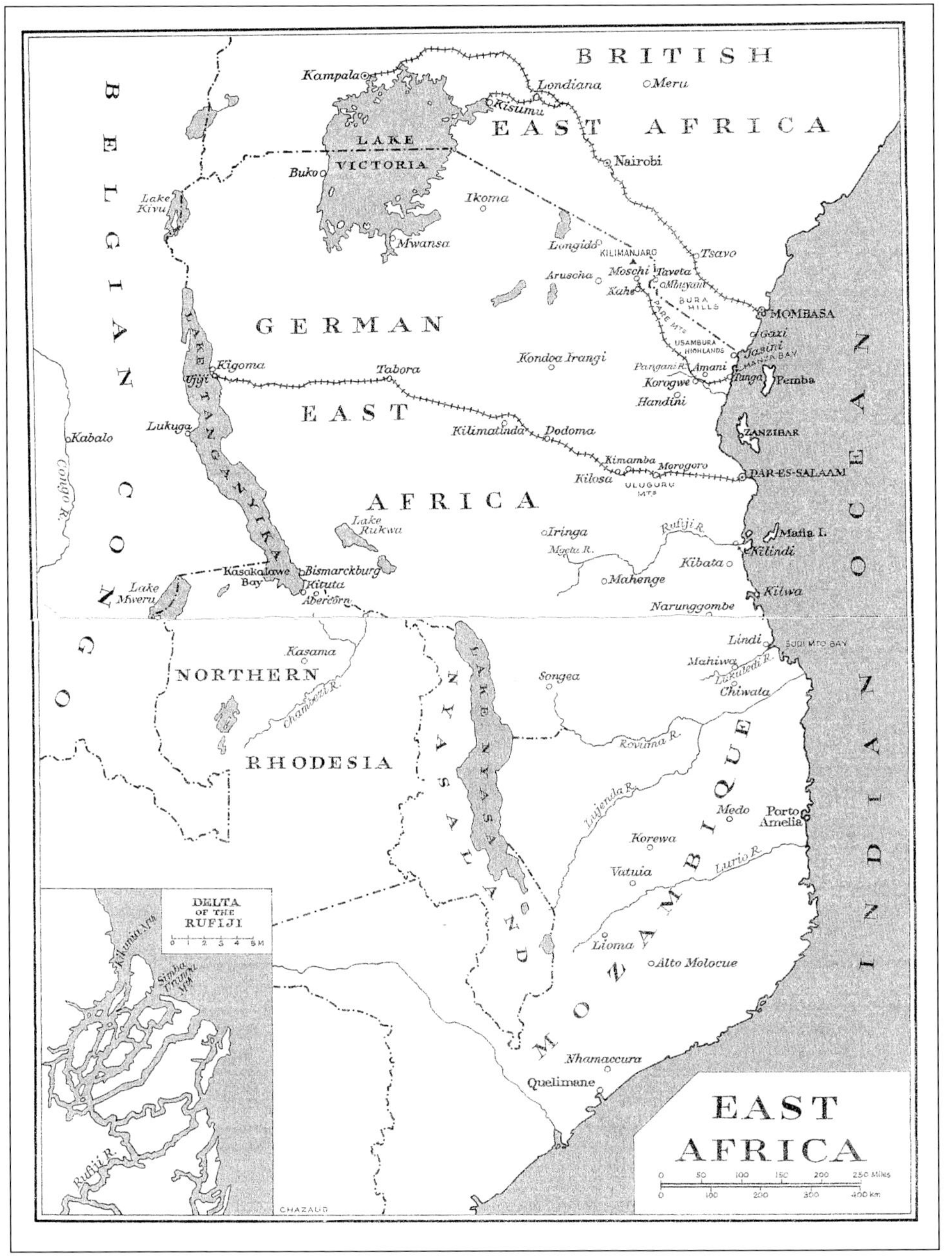

Map of East Africa

Schutztruppe für Ostafrika, Motitz Ruhl, Leipzig. N.D. Note the use of white piping on the Home Service and parade uniforms and cornflower blue on the khaki and white summer uniforms. The ordnance Ober-Büchsenmacher tunic is piped in red as seen in the following illustration.

Schutztruppe für Ostafrika, Ruhl.

Militär-Informations-Postkarten No.16 Kaiserliche Schutztruppen in Öst-Afrika. Carl Henckel, Pirma. 99 I/R; Askari Gefreiter; the red rank insignia (not visible) is worn on the left arm. He is armed with a Gew.M71 single-shot rifle. NCO in field uniform. Shown in this illustration are the tropenhelm, Kar.88, large water bottle, and canvas gaiters attached by six buckled straps. Senior Office-Station Chief. Dressed in a white summer uniform piped in cornflower blue. Feldwebel. In tropical dress uniform with white tropenhelm. In the background a Senior Ordnance Technician and a Medical Officer.

An example of an Askari NCO tarbusch (left) and an enlisted man (right) pictured in a catalog for a Jan Kube auction of Schutztruppen material in Germany.

Captain, Parade Home Service uniform. Note the white piping worn on this uniform. Uniformen der Marine und Schutztruppen. Waldorf Astoria.

Staff Doctor in tropical uniform. Uniformen der Marine Schutztruppen. Waldorf Astoria.

Major in summer dress. Uniformen der Marine Schutztruppen. Waldorf Astoria.

A pen and ink illustration by R.J. Marrion from the no longer published Tradition magazine. L: An Askari Sergeant with a grey felt hat trimmed in white, tan/brown drill material jacket and trousers piped in cornflower blue; rank and buttons in silver, puttees in grey/blue and brown boots. R: A Feldwebel in the white summer uniform of drill material piped in cornflower blue. The tropenhelm is decorated with a black, silver, and red national kokarde and the shoulder straps are white, red, and black mixture. His rank permits carrying an officer's pattern sword

General Paul Emil Von Lettow-Vorbeck. A colored lithographic poster designed by Fritz Grothemeyer in 1918 for fundraising for the "Colonial War Victim's Fund." The poster was executed in ochre, black and blue and features Lettow-Vorbeck on parade before ranks of marching Askaris. At the bottom is a bold facsimile of Lettow-Vorbeck's signature.

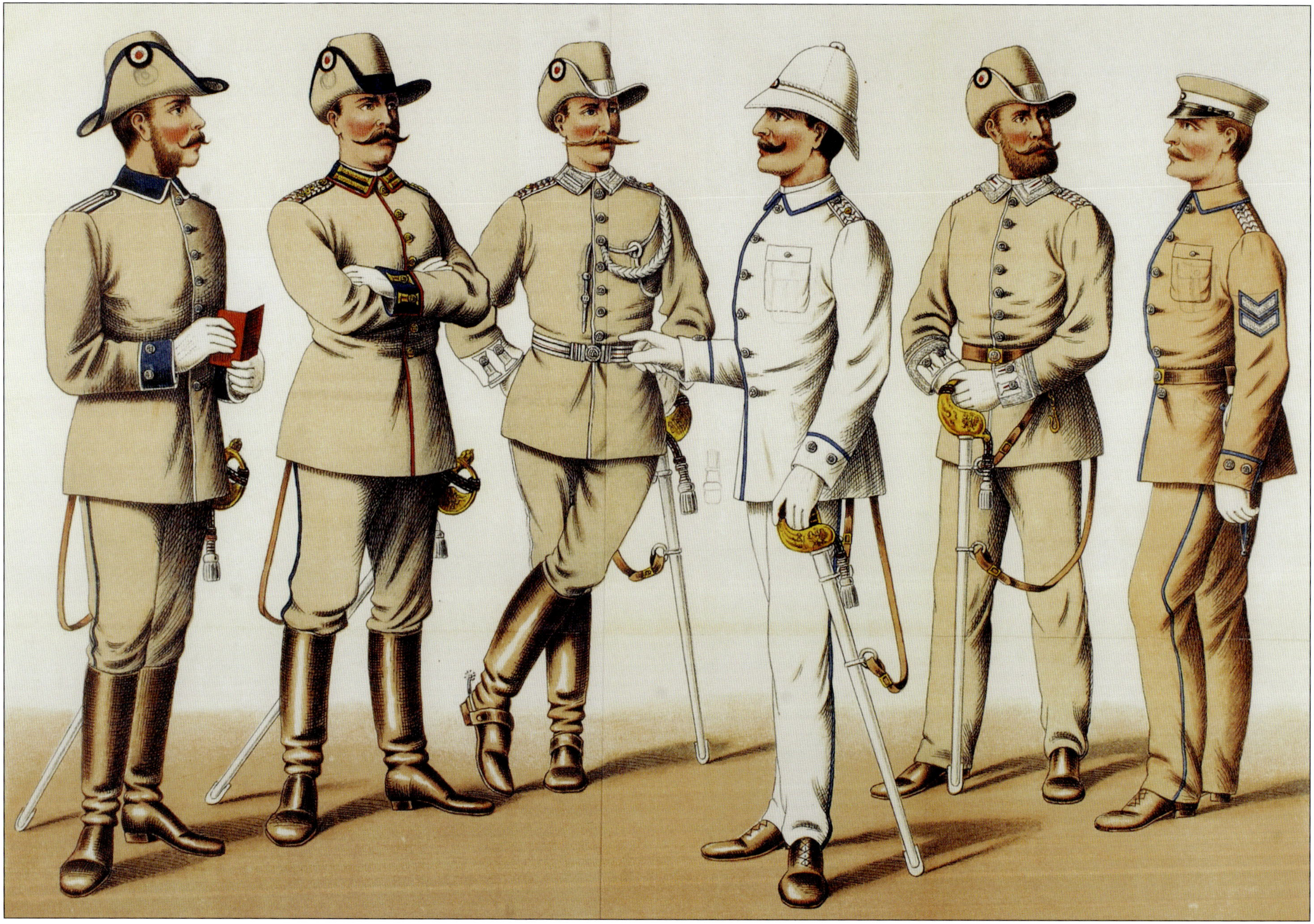

A Ruhl poster-sized illustration of Deutsch-Ostafrika Schutztruppen. L/R: Paymaster, Physician, Commissioned Officer, Officer in Tropical Uniform, Feldwebel, Sergeant.

Left: Schutztruppe Deutsch-Ostafrika, 1914. Oberleutnant in a cornflower blue-piped white tropical uniform; Hauptmann is in white-piped Kordwaffenrock. Zweifarben Tücher. Frederich Schirmer.

Right: Sanitäts-Unteroffizier (Medical) in the Kordwaffenrock of blue sand grey cord material; Sergeant in khakianzug. Note the red, white and black band on the tropenhelm, the blue piping on the uniform, and rank stripes. Zweifarben Tücher. Frederich Schirmer.

Medical NCO in what is captioned a Litewka. Uniformen der Marine Schutztruppen. From Waldorf Astoria.

Many European volunteers living in Deutsch-Ostafrika joined the Schutztruppe when war broke out in 1914. The figure on the left is in the uniform of that force, and is armed with a Gew.M71. The Hauptmann on the right is in the standard khaki field uniform. Zweifarben Tücher. Frederich Schirmer.

A Leutnant and a Vizefeldwebel from a mounted company. Note the khaki-colored legwraps worn by the NCO. Zweifarben Tücher. Frederich Schirmer.

A mounted sergeant of a "Berittene Komp." in the khaki field service uniform, with a Gew.M71 slung across his back. Zweifarben Tücher. Frederich Schirmer.

Schirmer evidenced a deep interest in the Askaris as shown in the following eleven illustrations from *Zweifarben Tücher.*

Five Askaris man a C/73 ship's gun. The C/73 was modified to fire smokeless ammunition and was reclassified as C/73/88. Zweibarben Tücher. Frederich Schirmer.

Right
Top: An Askari machine gun crew with a European NCO operating a Maxim MG 01. Note the large wheel fixed between the forward legs of the non-standard mount. This may have been intended to facilitate rapid redeployment of the gun when in the field. Zweifarben Tücher. Frederich Schirmer

Bottom: An Askari NCO wearing a colored scarf and a tribal modification of the tarbusch. The addition of grasses and a circular six-pointed design add considerably to the plain issue tarbusch. The enlisted man on the left shows hard service in the field with a torn and tattered uniform, lack of boots and a field-designed style of headgear. A photo of these tarbusch additions and modifications is shown in Charles Miller's Battle for the Bundu, facing page 213. Zweifarben Tücher. Frederich Schirmer.

Two Askari, one enlisted, the other a sergeant. Both have modified headgear with added grasses which were seen when the troops were actively in the field. Zweibarben Tücher. Frederich Schirmer.

An enlisted man and NCO signaling crew. Both show the signal specialty patch of crossed flags on the left sleeve. The signaler at the device has made a shield for his eyes by reversing his tarbusch and folding the neck flap under the cap to form a visor. Zweifarben Tücher. Frederich Schirmer.

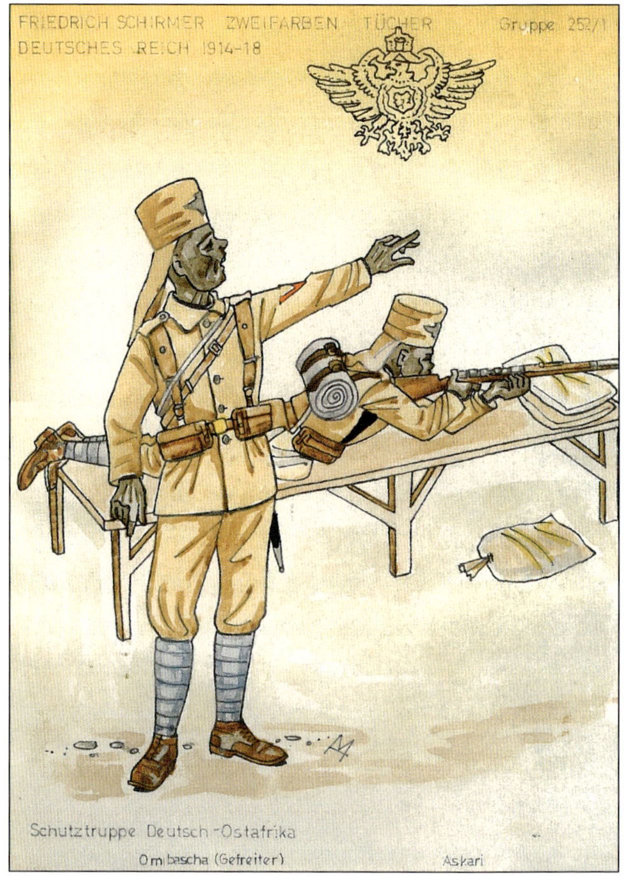

The Askari were the best trained of any of the native troops employed by any European country in Africa. They were trained in the same manner and discipline as were recruits in the Kaiser's Home Army. Depicted is target practice with the single-shot Gew.M71. Zweibarben Tücher. Frederich Schirmer.

A mounted Askari, painted by Ker., illustrates the small type of African ponies used by the Cavalry throughout the 1914-1918 campaign in Deutsch-Ostafrika. Zweibarben Tücher. Frederich Schirmer.

Another illustration by Ker. portrays an Askari Ombascha, or Gefreiter and a Sol, or Feldwebel, in field uniform. Zweifarben Tücher. Frederich Schirmer.

A colorful illustration from Zweifarben Tücher shows three Askari musicians, two trumpeters and a kettle drummer. The swallows-nest shoulder insignia are made of red, black, and white cotton. The crown and crossed swords insignia on the trumpet banners is an interesting, but unidentified detail. Zweibarben Tücher. Frederich Schirmer.

An illustration of a Schutztruppen crewed Schnellfeuergeschutz, or rapid firing gun. An officer with binoculars supervises the results. Zweifarben Tücher. Frederich Schirmer.

An enlisted Askari wearing grasses around his tarbusch and a "Hornist" with the musician's "schwalbennester" on his shoulders. Zweibarben Tücher. Frederich Schirmer.

Askari Feldwebel giving orders. Uniformen der Marine Schutztruppen. Waldorf Astoria.

Askari Schausch, or NCO signaler. Uniformen der Marine Schutztruppen. Waldorf Astoria.

Askari Ombascha, or Gefreiter, in field service uniform. Uniformen der Marine Schutztruppen. Waldorf Astoria.

Askari enlisted man in field service uniform. Uniformen der Marine Schutztruppen. Waldorf Astoria.

Polizeitruppe, Askari policeman. Note the red "P" on a white background worn on the left sleeve. Uniformen der Marine Schutztruppen. Waldorf Astoria.

Feldwebel, white summer uniform. Uniformen der Marine Schutztruppen, Waldorf Astoria.

Paul Pietsch illustrates an Askari Effendi officer and an Ombascha, or Gefreiter, for Major Eberhard Hettler's work Marineinfanterie und Schutztruppen.

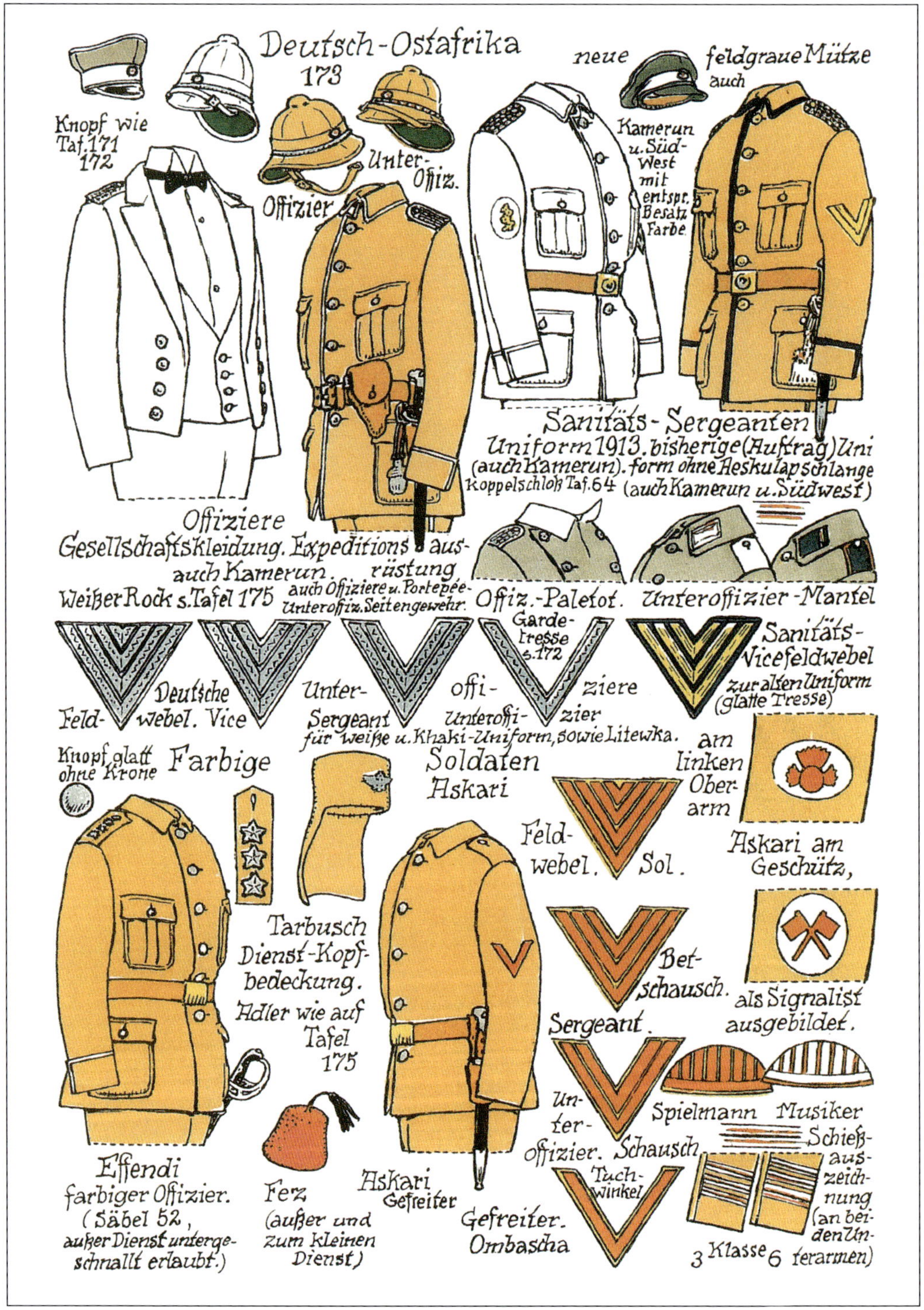

Deutsch-Ostafrika Uniforms and Insignia for German and native troops. Uniformenkunde Das Deutsches Heer. Paul Pietsch.

CHAPTER FOUR

Deutsche-Südwestafrika (German Southwest Africa)

The first Schutztruppe for Deutsch-Südwestafrika was established 1 May 1889. Its function was to provide armed protection against hostile forces, both internal and external, to the colony. This protection was for the rights of commercial enterprises and settlers, to safeguard against poachers, slave traders, smugglers, and any general unrest on the part of the natives against German interests. The first detachment consisted of one mounted battalion composed of two officers and twenty-one enlisted men who had volunteered from the Army as well as the Imperial Marines. Within five years, by 1894, the force had expanded and then functioned along the lines of the regular Army and consisted of:

1 Staff Officer, Commander and Governor of the Colony
1 Staff Officer, second in command, and Commander of the Schutztruppen
4 Captains
4 1st Lieutenants
18 2nd Lieutenants
5 Doctors
1 Veterinarian
6 Paymaster Assistants
142 NCOs
568 Enlisted men, including Corporals
750 Total European German forces

The division of the early forces was:

4 Field Companies
1 Field Artillery Battery
1 Construction Battalion

These forces were garrisoned throughout the Colony with the headquarters located centrally at Windhoek *(see map)*.

The force continued to grow, and by 1913 a re-organization took place that geographically broke the units into three commands. The *Headquarters Command* remained at Windhoek with the Command staff, Directory, Medical staff and Survey Troop. Also at Windhoek was the *Northern Command* that consisted of 1. Kompagnie, 4. Kompagnie (Machine Gun), 6. Kompagnie, 2. Batterie, Transport Train 1., Provisions Headquarters, and a Mount Depot. The *Southern Area Command* was a larger force and consisted of 2. and 3. Kompagnie, 5. Kompagnie (Machine Gun), 7. Kompagnie (camel riders and machine gun), 8. Kompagnie and Lazarett (hospital) Kompagnie stationed together, 9. Kompagnie, 1.

Batterie, 3. Batterie, Artillery and Train Depots, Clothing Depot, Garrison Administration, Mount Station and camel storage and breeding center. These individual units were dispersed to sixteen locations within the Colony.

By 1913, the combined German strength of the above units had grown to:

90 Officers
22 Doctors
9 Veterinarians
59 Military officials, ordnance, etc.
342 NCOs
1444 Enlisted men

These statistics did not include native troops. Schutztruppen reported to the Reichs Colonial Office. The additional force of Polizeitruppen was responsible to the Colonial Civil Authorities and consisted of:

7 Officers
9 Head Administrators
68 Police Senior Sergeants
432 Police Sergeants
50 Hired Supervisors for the native police

Deutsch-Südwestafrika Schutztruppen uniforms were as follows.

The Waffenrock of the Heimaths-Uniform was in the style of the regular Prussian army; however, it had a foldover collar instead of a standing one. The cuffs were Swedish-pattern each with two silver litzen and buttons. The collar bore double litzen which ran nearly halfway around the collar. The base color for the cuffs and collar was cornflower blue, the same as the piping which ran down the front of the tunic and the edges of the flaps in the rear. The tunic itself was generally made of a whipcord-type wool and the color was referred to as "sand grey". The buttons were silver and bore the Imperial Crown. The tunic had hidden pockets inside the rear flaps and the inside breast, but there were no outside pockets. Riding breeches were worn and were piped along the outer seam in cornflower blue. The boots worn with this uniform were brown leather with silver spurs.

The epaulets were in the Army pattern with red and black threads in place of the normal State colors commonly found on standard Army issues. The Waffenrock with a brocade belt in silver bullion with red, silver, and black stripes running horizontally with a buckle bearing the Imperial Crown was worn primarily on parade. In parade order a silver Officers Aigulette having flecks in red, silver, and black interwoven was worn on the left side of the tunic. For parade dress, white gloves were worn, as was the Officer's pattern sword with silver portepee.

The hat was of fine grey felt and had a wide brim turned up and fastened on the right side with a large red white and black Deutsches kokarde. The hat was piped along the outer edges with a 3 1/2cm. band of cornflower blue; the center band was also in this color, 12cm. in width.

The mütze, or cap, was the same form as worn by the Prussian Army and made of sand grey "Cord-Stoff", the color of the Waffenrock. The piping and cap band were cornflower blue material; the leather trim was dark brown. It is interesting to note that in the earlier period of Colonial service, prior to 1902, the 1893/95 model kepi was worn both by officers and enlisted men. It was trimmed in cornflower blue, as were the later mützen. The kepi is illustrated in the first series of the Ruhl plates, while the second series illustrates the typical later-styled mütze.

The Officer's Home Service Pattern uniform varied slightly from the Waffenrock. The color was the same; the collars and cuffs were plain with no litzen and no cornflower blue, although cornflower blue piping outlined the plain cuff and collar. Either straight-leg trousers or riding breeches could be worn with this uniform; boots and other leather accessories were in brown leather. The felt-brimmed hat, or mütze, could be worn with a single Reichs kokarde on the right side of the hat, or in the center of the mütze.

The Kordwaffenrock was a field uniform made of tan cord cotton material cut like the Waffenrock with all insignia piping and buttons the same. The brimmed hat, riding breeches and brown boots were most commonly worn.

By order of 28 November 1899, for combat conditions a "Kord-Feldrock", or "Kord-litewka", was worn. The cut of the tunic varied from those previously described. There was no color piping; the buttons were hidden; there were two flapped breast pockets. The rank insignia remained the same. The felt-brimmed hat was worn with brown leather equipment that consisted of a field belt, binocular case, map case, pistol holster, and a short side arm (bayonet-style) with portepee.

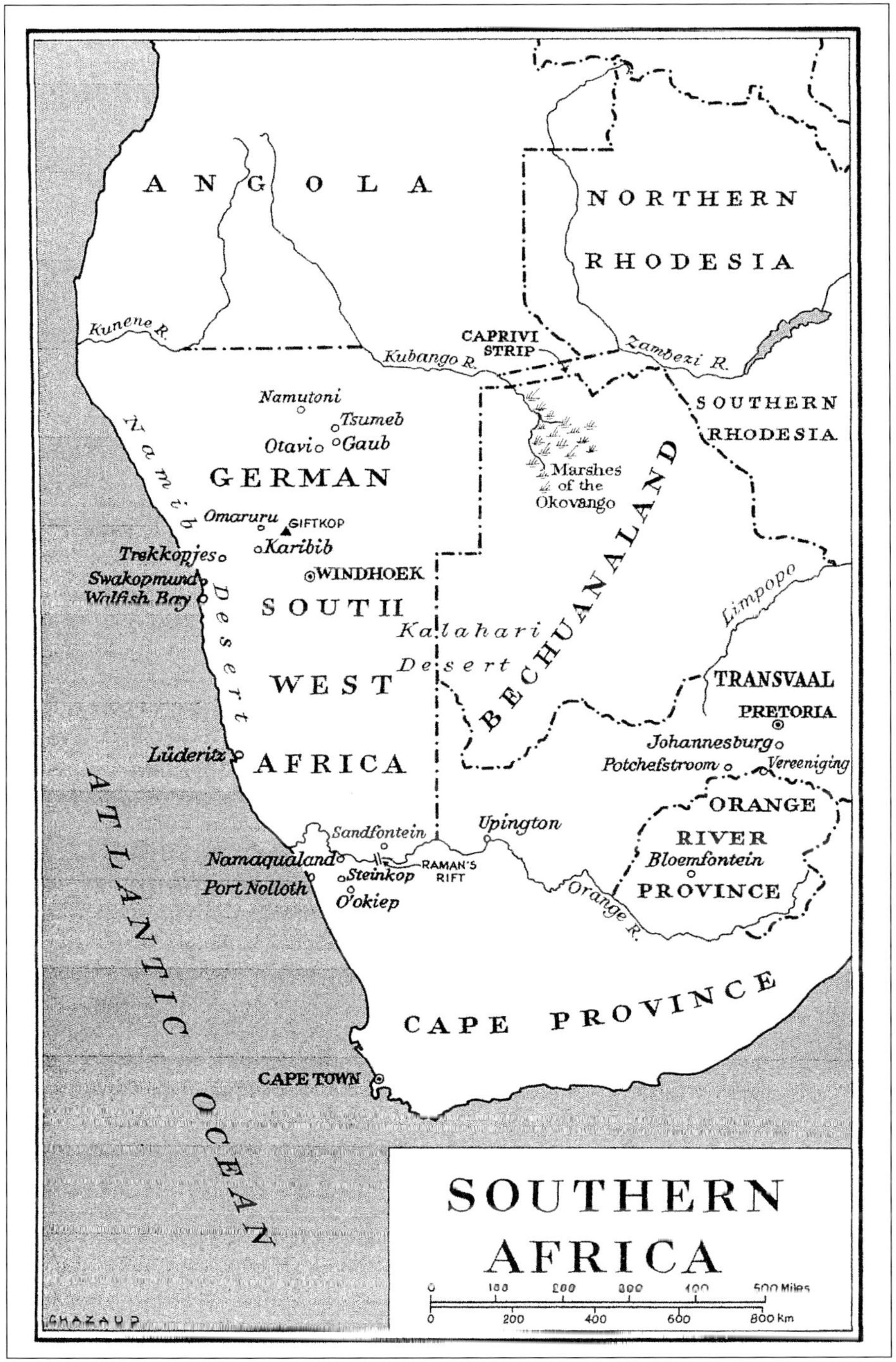

Map of Southern Africa including Deutsch-Südwestafrika.

An officer wearing the "Kordwaffenrock". During the period, 1893-1895, the cord jacket was sand grey with cornflower blue collar, cuffs, and piping. Buttons, shoulder straps, lace and Aiguilette were silver, as was the sash which was highlighted with red and black thread. The breeches were the same color as the jacket, also of cord, with cornflower blue piping. This officer wears the kepi in grey with blue piping and band and dark leather visor. The illustration, by R.J. Marrion, appeared in the excellent and now, sadly, no longer published Tradition magazine.

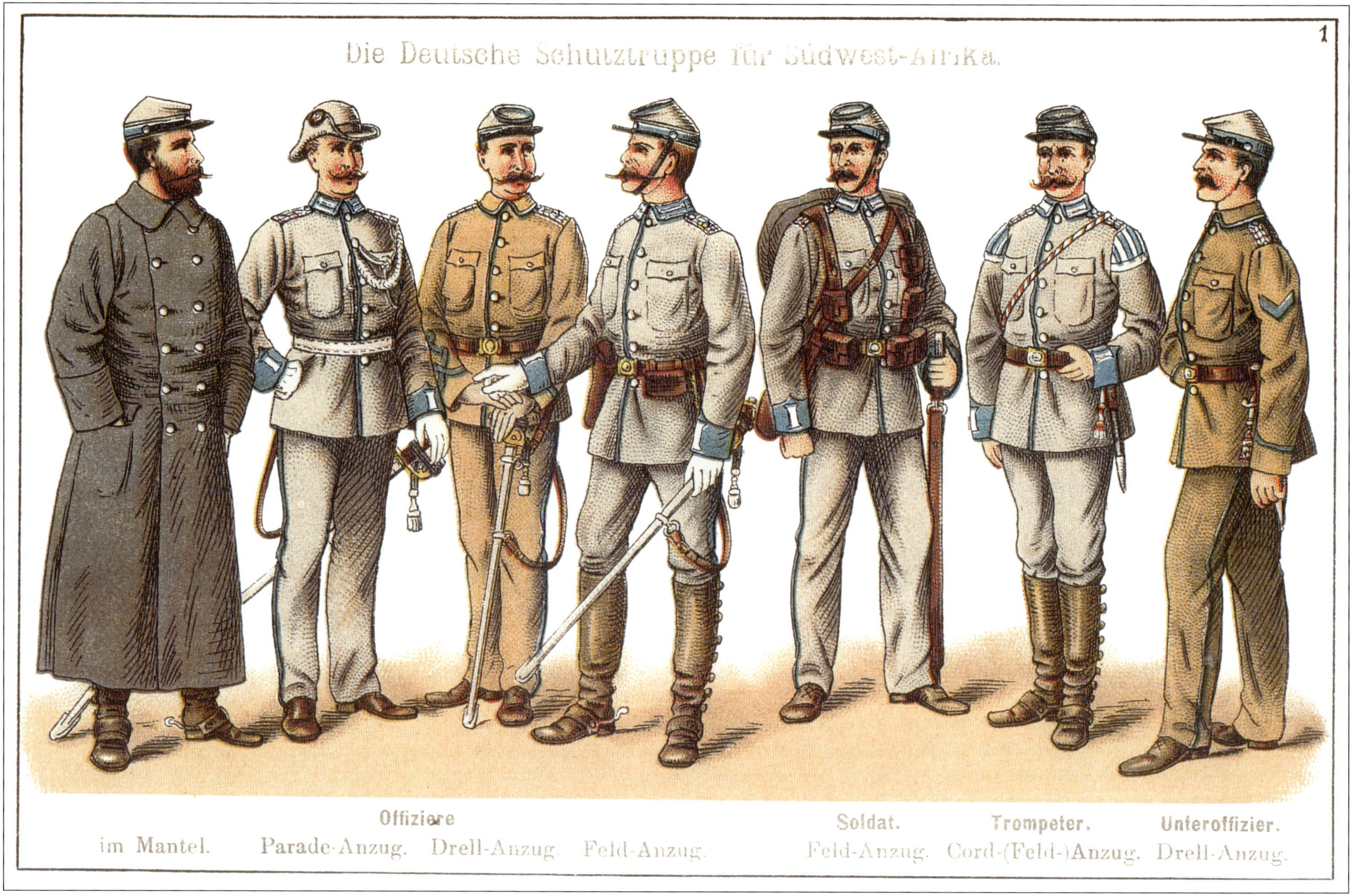

Südwest-Afrika Schutztruppe. Of particular interest in this plate and the following from the first edition of Deutsche Schutztruppen für Südwest-Afrika, Verlag von Moritz Ruhl, Leipzig, N.D., are the kepis worn both by officers and enlisted men until c.1895 when the mütze became standard issue.

It is interesting to note that Ruhl in this first and in the following edition of Deutsche Schutztruppen für Südwest-Afrika, Verlag von Moritz Ruhl, Leipzig, N.D., did not include any illustrations of Askari uniforms.

Ruhl's second edition of the Deutsche Schutztruppen für Südwest-Afrika book. Note some of the subtle changes: kepi to mütze; added collar tabs; straight leg trousers to riding breeches, to name a few. Descriptions for this page are identical to those on page 46.

From the second edition of Ruhl's Deutsche Schutztruppen für Südwest-Afrika. Descriptions for this page are identical to those on page 47.

A senior Veterinarian in Home Service dress from Uniformen der Marine und Schutztruppen. Waldorf Astoria, Munchen, c.1924.

Oberleutnant in paletot, or greatcoat. Uniformen der Marine und Schutztruppen. Waldorf Astoria.

Hauptmann, General Staff in grey cord uniform. Uniformen der Marine und Schutztruppen. Waldorf Astoria.

Tropenuniformen in Südwestafrika. L/R Mounted Unterofficier, Officier and Station Chief, Schutztruppe Cavalry in dismounted order, Trompeter in "Station dress". Militär-Informations-Postkarten No.17., Militär Kunst Verlag Mars, Pirma, Dresden.

A mounted Cavalryman in field marching order. A print from the extensive series Zweifarben Tücher produced by Schirmer, illustration by Ker.

A Gefreiter Trumpeter in a sand grey Waffenrock and brown leather "patronengürtels 94" (cartridge boxes), and belting. A Unteroffizier is shown in khaki, with the "patronengürtels 94", Gew.98, and Seitengewher 98 with a Colonial swordknot. Zweifarben Tücher. Frederich Schirmer.

The Schutztruppe field batteries were widely equipped with the light 7.5cm. Mountain Howitzer L/17 of 1908. This drawing by Ker. illustrates the gun and its six man crew in firing position, c.1914.

From Frederich Schirmer's Zweifarben Tücher is this illustration by Ker. of a Kamelreiter in the khaki field uniform. Note the cornflower blue piping on the collar, cuffs and tunic front.

Ruhl published a series of large uniform plates in a poster format. The purpose or use of this large size format is obscure, but possibly they were displayed in military kasernes, or public buildings. This example depicts uniforms of Deutsch-Südwestafrika. L/R Rossart, officier, officier, Sänitats (medical), unteroffizier, and spielleute (musician).

Mounted trooper in the khaki field uniform. Uniformen der Marine und Schutztruppen. Waldorf Astoria.

Trumpeter-Gefreiter in walking-out Home Service uniform. Uniformen der Marine und Schutztruppen. Waldorf Astoria.

From Schirmer, a Feldwebel in Ordannanzanzug and a Cavalry trooper in the Home Service uniform, both made of sand grey cord material.

Paul Pietsch illustrates a Vize-Feldwebel in the Home Service uniform and an Etm-Feldwebel in the tropical uniform with a pith sun helmet. Marineinfanterie und Schutztruppen. Major Eberhard Hettler.

Pietsch illustrates the "Kord" uniforms worn in "Süd-West Afrika". Uniformenkunde Das Deutsche Heer.

Leutnant, cord field service uniform. Uniformen der Marine und Schutztruppen. Waldorf Astoria.

Oberleutnant and Adjutant, khaki field uniform. Uniformen der Marine und Schutztruppen. Waldorf Astoria.

Feldwebel, "ordinary" uniform. Uniformen der Marine und Schutztruppen. Waldorf Astoria.

Unteroffizier, winter greatcoat. Uniformen der Marine und Schutztruppen. Waldorf Astoria.

Landespolizei Sergeant in light patrol uniform. Uniformen der Marine und Schutztruppen. Waldorf Astoria.

Landespolizei, Polizeiwachmeister, field patrol uniform. Uniformen der Marine und Schutztruppen. Waldorf Astoria.

CHAPTER FIVE

Ostasiatischen Expedition Korps (East Asiatic Expedition Corps)

For service in the Pacific German held colonies, the Ostasiatischen Expedition Korps was established by "Kaiserliche Order vom 8. Juli 1900" and consisted of the following units:

1st Ostasiatische Infanterie–Brigade made up of 1st Ostasiatische Infanterie-Regiment consisting of 2 Bataillonen with four companies each and of a ninth company created from the Garde and III. ArmeeKorps, plus the VI., XI., and XVIII. ArmeeKorps. 2nd Ostasiatisches Infanterie-Regiment consisting of 2 Bataillonen each with four companies and a ninth created from the VI., XII., XIX., and from IV., XI., and XVIII, ArmeeKorps.

2nd Ostasiatische Infanterie-Brigade made up of 3rd Ostasiatisches Infanterie-Regiment of 2 Bataillonen of four companies each and a ninth company created from II., IX., X., plus men from VII., VIII., and XIII. ArmeeKorps. 4th Ostasiatisches Infanterie-Regiment, 2 Bataillonen each with four companies and a ninth created from XIV., XV., XVI., and the Bavarian I., II., and III. ArmeeKorps.

3rd Ostasiatische Infanterie-Brigade made up of 5th Ostasiatisches Infanterie-Regiment of 2 Bataillonen four companies, plus a ninth company. 6th Ostasiatisches Infanterie-Regiment of 2 Bataillonen of four companies, plus, as with the other regiments, an additional ninth company.

The Ostasiatische Jäger-Kompagnie

The Ostasiatische Reiter-Regiment, consisting of four mounted squadrons.

The Ostasiatische-Feld-Artillerie Regiment, consisting of three detachments with three field batteries each.

The Ostasiatisches Bataillon Schwerer Feldhaubitzen, with two batteries of heavy artillery.

Ostasiatisches Pioniere-Bataillon, consisting of three companies.

Ostasiatisches Eisenbahn-Bataillon, consisting of three Eisenbahn-Kompagnien.

The Ostasiatischen Expedition Korps was further supplemented by a telegraph section, a sanitary or medical company, a munitions column, and the other varied personnel and minor units necessary to the functioning of the Expedition Korps.

Weapons, Equipment and Uniforms of the Ostasiatischen Troops

Infantry

As previously described, the Ostasiatischen Infanterie-Regimenter were made up of 2 Bataillonen of four companies each and a ninth company which was included as a substitute company, or for rear area service.

The basic weapon was the "Infanterie-Gewehr M 98" of 7.92 mm and the bayonet Seitengewehr M 98 n.A. The cool weather uniform consisted of a dark blue Litewka with red collar patches on a turned down collar. White shoulder straps were worn with red regimental embroidered numbers. Grey-black trousers with red piping, leather boots, a cap and helmet of the infantry pattern completed the uniform. The summer uniform, a tunic with six buttons, trousers, and schurmützen, or caps, was made of green-gold cotton material. The shoulder straps were as worn on the Litewka. A woven straw hat, *Strohhüte*, was off-white, with a natural leather chinstrap. The brim was turned up on the right side and was held by a large national kokarde. Also worn was a smaller state kokarde for the soldier's home station. The boots were brown canvas and leather.

The overcoat was grey wool with white shoulder straps with red regimental numbers. The equipment was of the latest pattern, complete with pack, ground sheet, mess kit, canteen and breadbag of brown canvas and hung from a belt under the field pack. The soldier was also equipped with a tri-cote washable bedcover and mosquito netting.

A recommended list of equipment and uniforms for officers of the Ostasiatische Expedition Korps from *Unsere Truppen in Ost-Asien*, Zweite Auflage, consisted of *Strohhüte*, Litewka, one pair of trousers for high boots, one pair of tall boots with double soles, necktie, one pair of infantry-style epaulets with regimental numbers attached, a sword, portepee, sword belt, one pair of brown gloves, a revolver and holster, field glasses with case, a signaling whistle with chain, a map case, pencils, a compass with case, a leather purse, a helmet, two mützen, or caps, two light brown drill tropical weight Litewka, two pair of shoes, one pair of long tropical trousers, a warm vest, a leather jacket, a paletot, or overcoat, four pair of woolen gloves, a sleeping bag, mosquito netting, a tobacco pipe and tobacco pouch, a canteen, and other mess equipment for the field.

Cavalry

The Ostasiatische Reiter-Regiment consisted of four squadrons with a total strength of 800 men. All personnel carried the cavalry sabre of an unspecified model and the Karbiner 98a. The cavalry Litewka was grey with red collar tabs and shoulder straps. The trousers were a blue-black without piping. Boots were of the high riding style with spurs. The field cap was green with a red band. Note in the following illustration that the field cap is shown in blue with a red band. The helmet was the design of the 1.Garde-Dragoner-Regiment. The overcoat was grey with red collar tabs and shoulder straps. The summer uniform was of the same green-gold drill material as worn by other branches, with red collar tabs and shoulder straps. The *Shrohhüte* was as worn by all troops. Other equipment consisted of a sword with belt and brown natural leather ammunition pouches. The officers were equipped as the infantry.

Feld-Artillerie-Regiment

The Feld-Artillerie-Regiment was made up of three Abteilungen (sections) of three batteries each. Each battery had six guns and three munition wagons. The Schwerer Feldhaubitzen Bataillon was staffed identically to the Feld-Artillerie-Regiment and consisted of two batteries, six guns, and 176 men. The Feld-Artillerie Regiment was armed with bayonets initially, and later, revolvers, while the Fuss-Artillerie was armed with the infantry weapon Gew.88 or Gew.98. Uniforms consisted of a blue Litewka with black collar patches and red shoulder straps with a gold embroidered grenade and battery numbers. The mütze and helmet were like the Prussian Artillery regiments. The mantel was grey with insignia the same as the Litewka. The summer uniform was identical to the other branches with red shoulder straps and gold grenades. Officers were dressed no differently than the infantry.

Pioniere und Verkehrstruppen

The Pioniere Bataillon and the Eisenbahn (railroad) Bataillon were made up of three companies each and attached with them was a Korps-Telegraphen-Abteilung (section). These units were uniformed identically to the Artillery, but with black shoulder straps with red trim.

Train-Abteilungen

The train detachment consisted of three Proviant-Kolonnen (food), three Feld-Bäckerei- Kolonnen (field bakery), and six Feld-Lazarethen-Kolonnen (field ambulance). Uniforms were identical to other branches, with the exception of light blue shoulder straps and a light blue-banded mütze. The medical corps wore the same Litewka and Drillichrock (lightweight drill uniform) as worn by the infantry, but with dark blue shoulder straps and collar patches.

Feldpost Personnel

This unit consisted of a postmaster, seven field post assistants, three postal guards, and two mounted deliverymen. The Feldpostbeamten were armed with a sword and revolver; the Unterbeamten with an infantry bayonet and a carbine; the mounted men were issued cavalry swords and revolvers. Nine Trainsoldaten were attached to the unit.

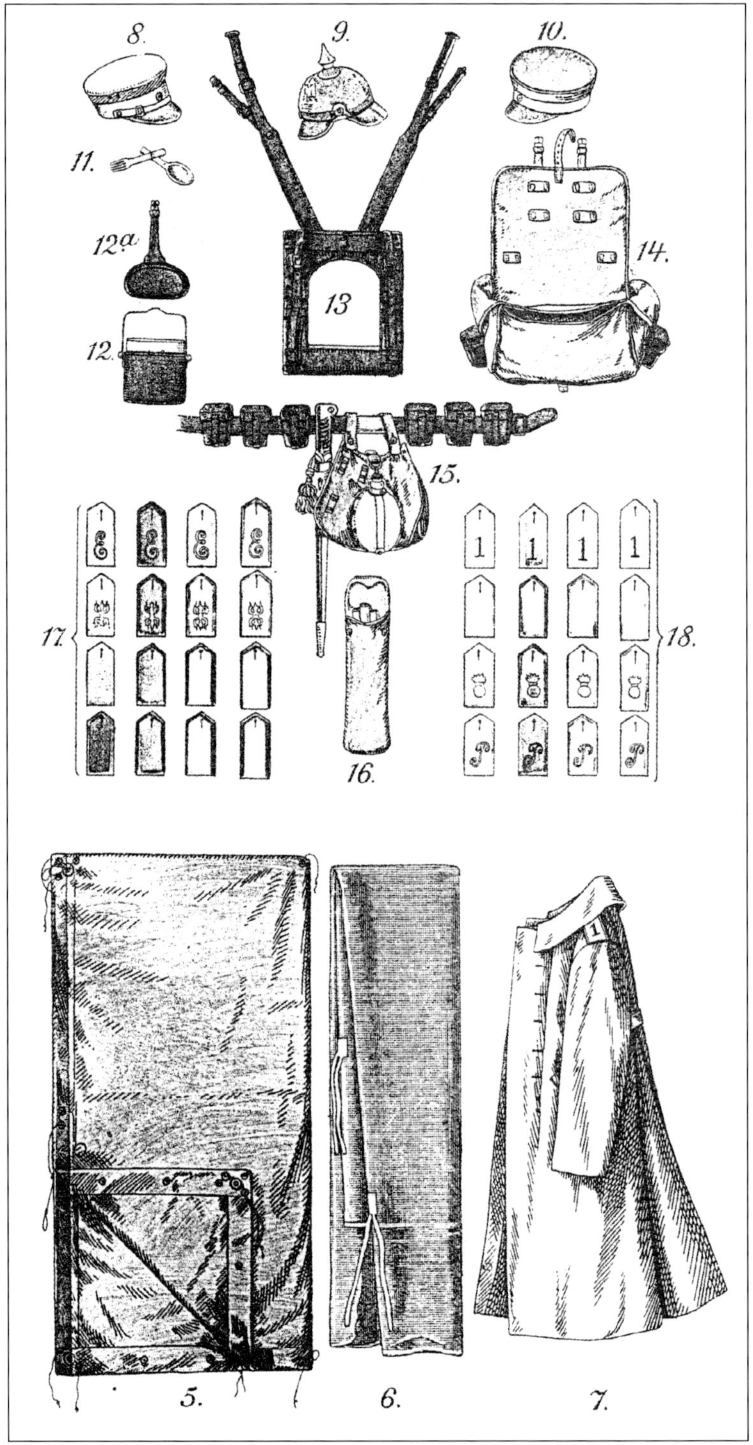

Right:
Tafel B. Equipment of the Ostasiatischen Brigade: Drawings are: 5 – Zeltbahn, 6 – Mosquito Netting, 7 – Overcoat, 8 – Summer Cap, 9 – Winter Helmet, 10 – Winter Cap, 11 – Knife and Fork, 12 – Mess Tin, 12a – Cover for Mess Tin, 13 – Backpack Frame, 14 – Pack, 15 – Service Belt with Cartridge Boxes, Breadbag, Canteen, and Bayonet, 16 – Tent Pegs for Zeltbahn, 17 and 18 – Shoulder Straps.

Opposite:
Tafel A. Illustrates the summer and winter uniforms as officially prescribed to by Veröffentlichungen aus dem Gebiete des Militär-Sanitätswesens 1904 (Military Hygiene Command). Drawings One and Two are of summer uniforms; three and four are of winter uniforms.

Tafel A: *Anzugsarten der Ostasiatischen Besatzungs-Brigade (aus: Veröffentlichungen aus dem Gebiete des Militär-Sanitätswesens 1904)*

1u.2. Sommeruniform.
3u.4. Winteruniform.
5. Zeltbahn.
6. Moskitonetz.
7 Mantel.

8. Sommermütze.
9. Winterhelm.
10. Wintermütze.
11. Essbesteck.
12. Kochgeschirr.

12a Deckel des Kochgeschirrs mit Handgriff.
13. Tragegerüst mit Trageriemen.
14. Gepäcksack mit seitlich angebrachten Patronentaschen.

15. Leibriemen mit Patronentaschen, Brotbeutel, Feldflasche u. Seitengewehr.
16. Zeltzubehörbeutel (mit Inhalt).
17u.18. Achselklappen.

Offiziere des Ostasiatischen Expeditionskorps.

Arzt in Litewka mit Strohhut. — **Pionier-Offizier** in Litewka mit Mütze. — **Artillerie-Offizier** in Litewka mit Mütze. — **Kavallerie-Offizier** in Litewka mit Strohhut. — **Generalmajor** in Litewka mit Mütze. — **Generalstabs-Offizier** in Litewka mit Mütze. — **Offizier vom I. Ostasiat. Inf.-Reg** in Litewka mit Helm.

Officers of the Ostasiatischen Expedition Korps. Unsere Truppen in Ost-Asien. Verlag Moritz Ruhl. Leipzig.

Ostasiatische Infanterie-Regimenter and Marine-Infanterie (See-Bataillon). Unsere Truppen in Ost-Asien. Verlag Moritz Ruhl. Leipzig.

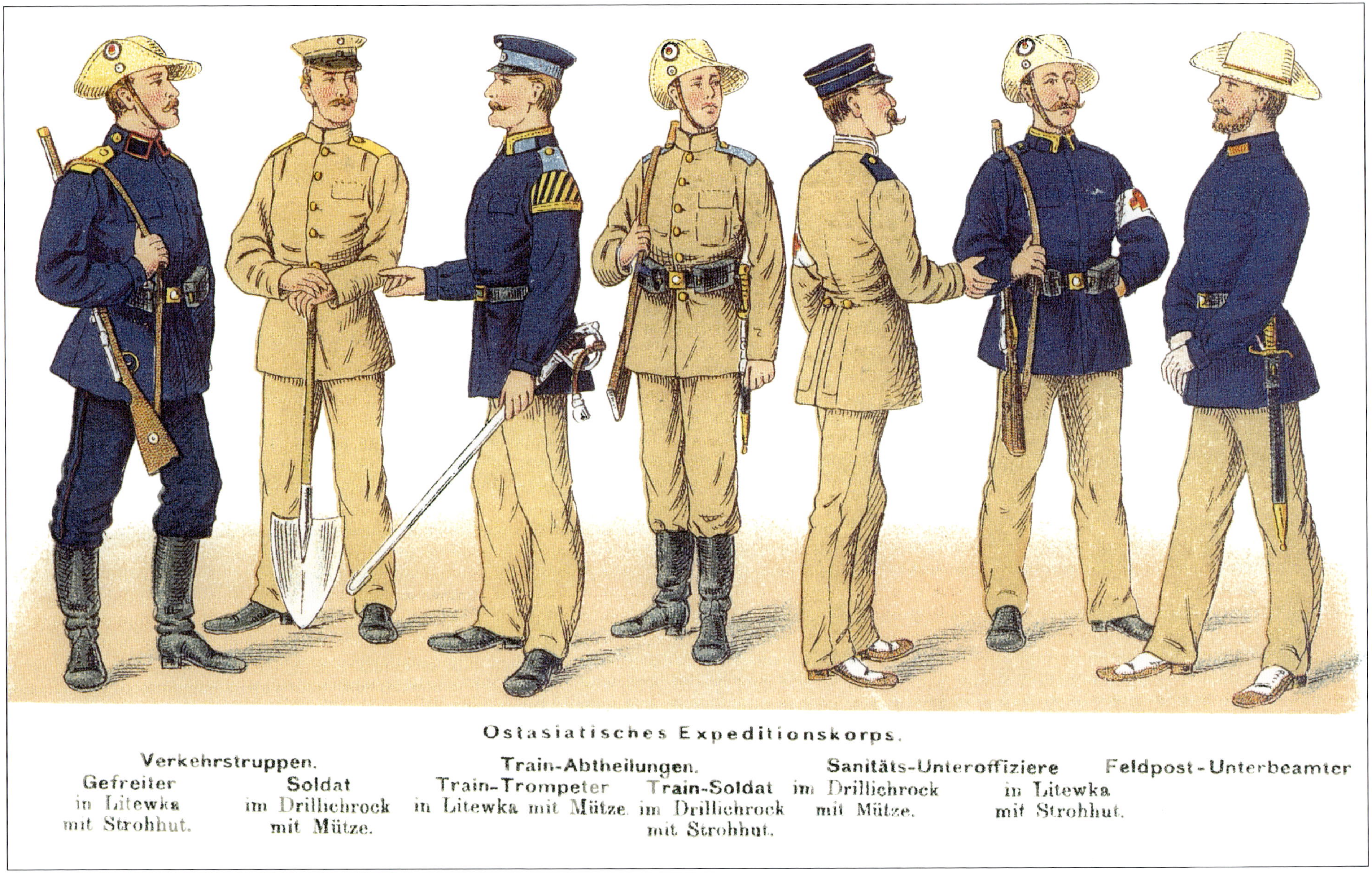

Ostasiatische Verkehrstruppen (Work Troops), Train-Abtheilungen (Train), Sanitäts-Unteroffizier (Hospital), and Feldpost-Unterbeamter (Postal). Unsere Truppen in Ost-Asien. Verlag Moritz Ruhl. Leipzig.

Ostasiatisches Reiter Regiment (Cavalry), Unteroffizier der Marine-Feldbatterie (Marine Artillery), Ostasiatisches Artillerie-Regiment (Artillery) and Ostasiatisches Pionier-Bataillon (Pioneer Troops). Unsere Truppen in Ost Asien. Verlag Moritz Ruhl. Leipzig.

Gefreiter Ostasiatische Marine Detachment in brown drill field uniform. Uniformen der Marine und Schutztruppen. Waldorf Astoria.

Right:
Infantrymen in brown summer drill uniforms, Gew. 98 rifles, Seitengewehr M 98 n.A bayonets and straw hats. Zeitschrift für Heereskunde.

Opposite
Left: Paul Pietsch illustrates Ostasiatisches Expedition Korps Infanterie Uniforms. L/R: 1900 Litweka, tropical summer uniform, 1901 winter Home Service uniform. Der Standhafte Zinnsoldat, Uniformenblatt Nr.28.

Right: The Expedition Korps Mountain Artillery. An officer in blue Litewka; another in summer weight field uniform. In the right background, an NCO directs the artillery crew. A. Schäfer, Der Standhafte Zinnsoldat, Uniformenblatt Nr.49.

„DER STANDHAFTE ZINNSOLDAT", Uniformenblatt Nr. 28
Ostasiatisches Expeditionskorps (Infanterie)
1900
Tropenkleidung
1901
Text in Heft 8 1937, Folge 119, — Herausgegeben von Joachim Ritter, Markkleeberg 1 bei Leipzig.

„DER STANDHAFTE ZINNSOLDAT" Uniformenblatt Nr. 49
Deutschland 1900—1901
I. 43
A. Schäfer
Ostasiatisches Expeditionskorps, Gebirgsartillerie,
Offiziere, Unteroffiziere, Artilleristen
Verl. d. Zeitschr. „Der Standhafte Zinnsoldat", Herausg. Joachim Ritter, Leipzig-Markkleeberg 1

The German military history journal Zeitschrift für Heereskunde ran several articles regarding the equipment and uniforms of the Ostasiatische Expedition Korps. Tafel A (below) depicts the M1900 winter uniform for enlisted men, the feldmütze for both enlisted and officers, a neck protector and three views of the blouse.

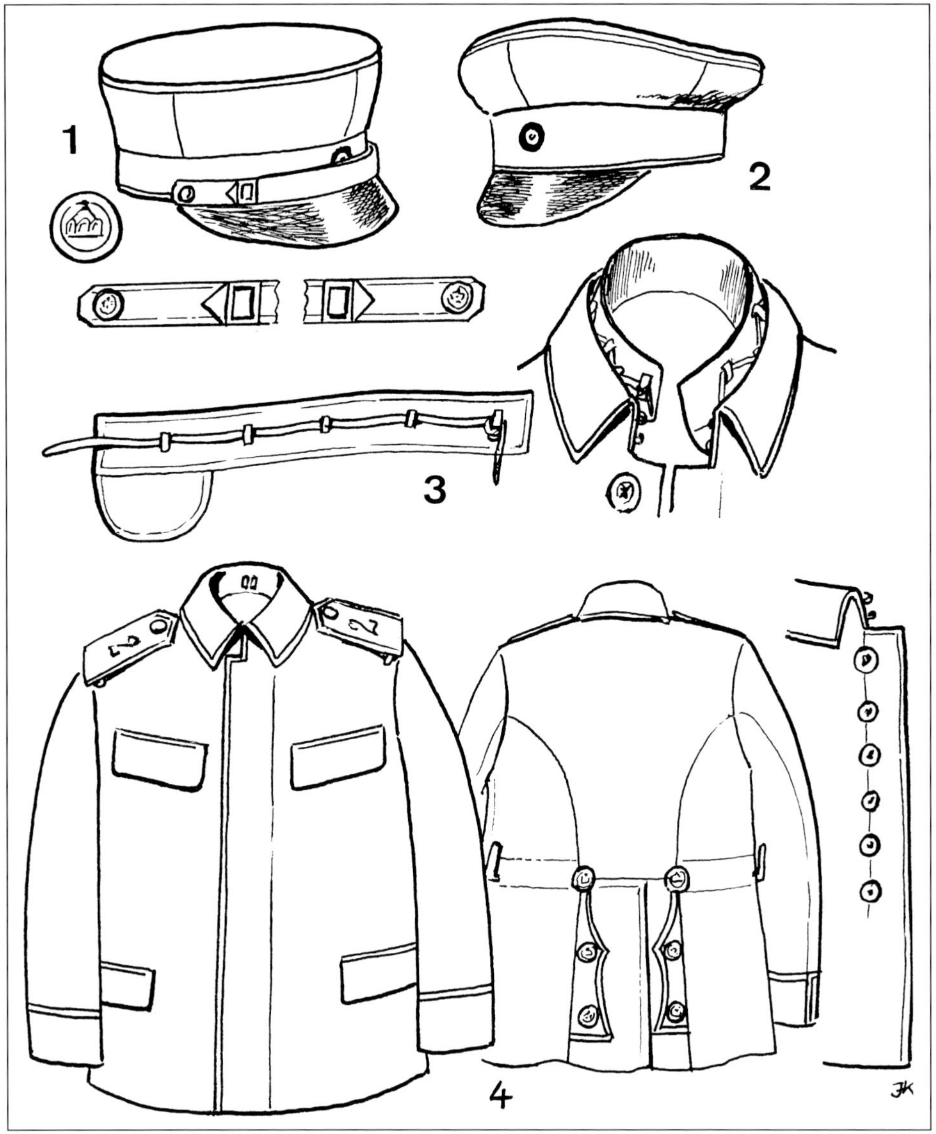

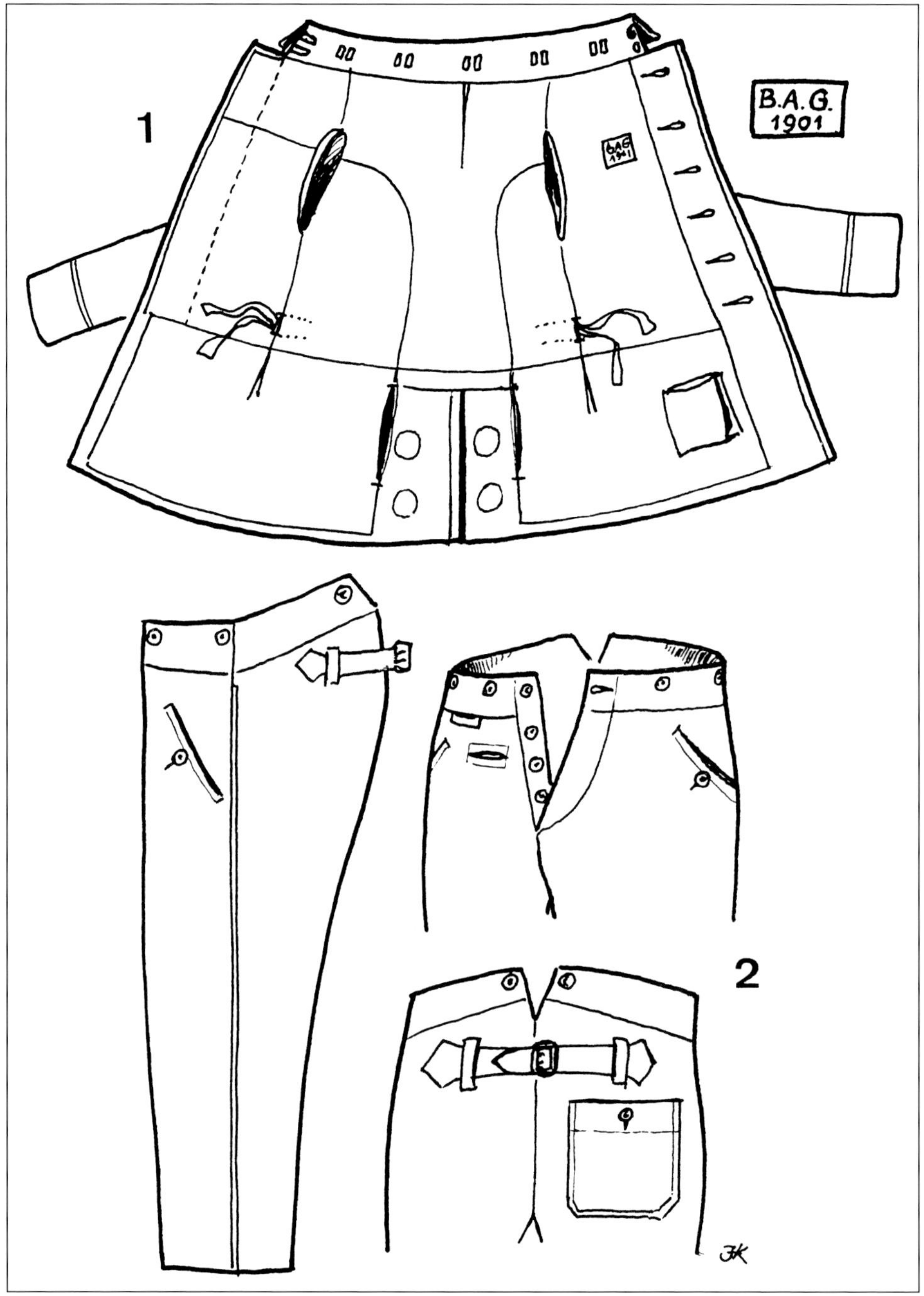

Tafel B. Details the interior of the winter blouse and trousers for foot troops.

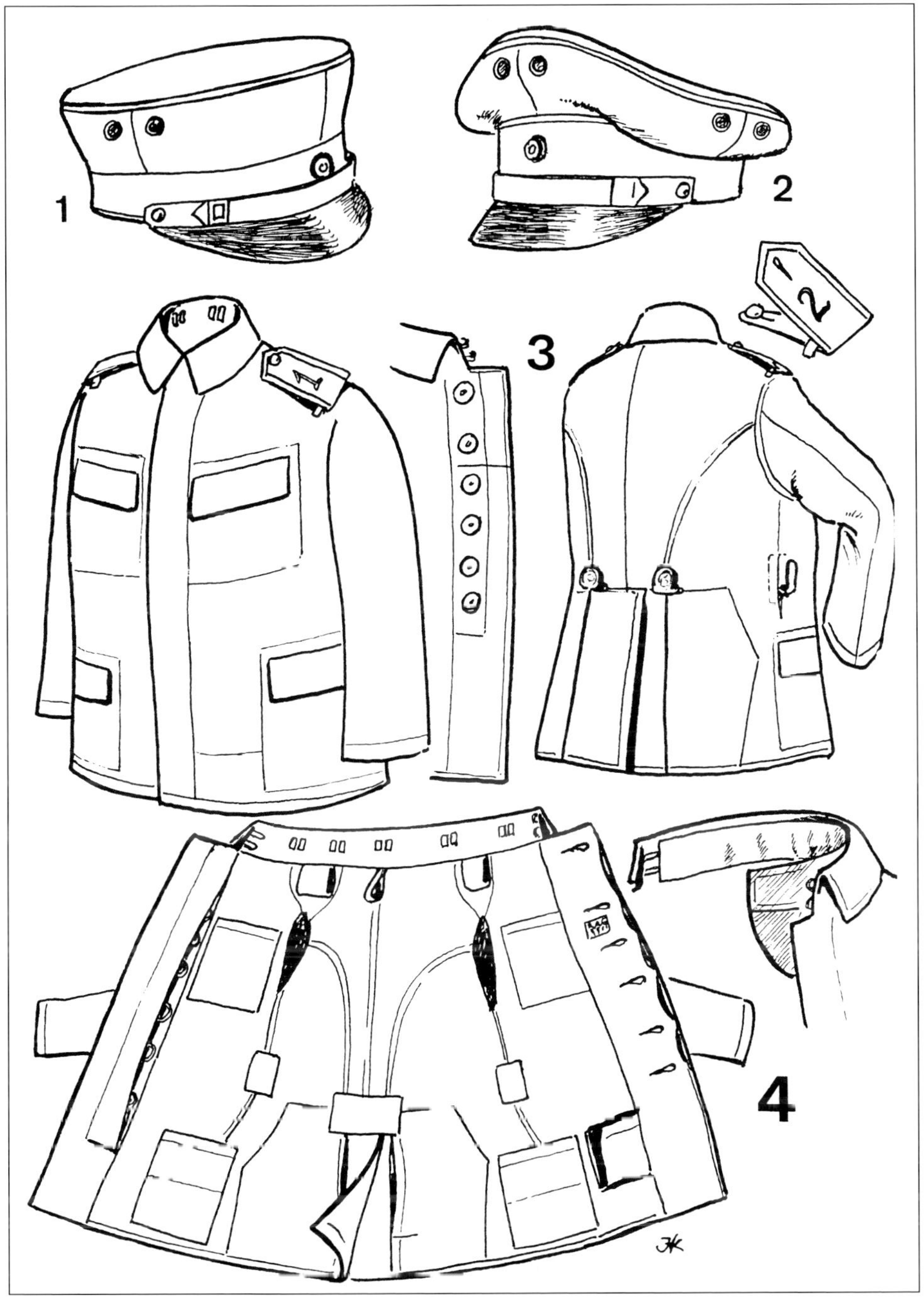

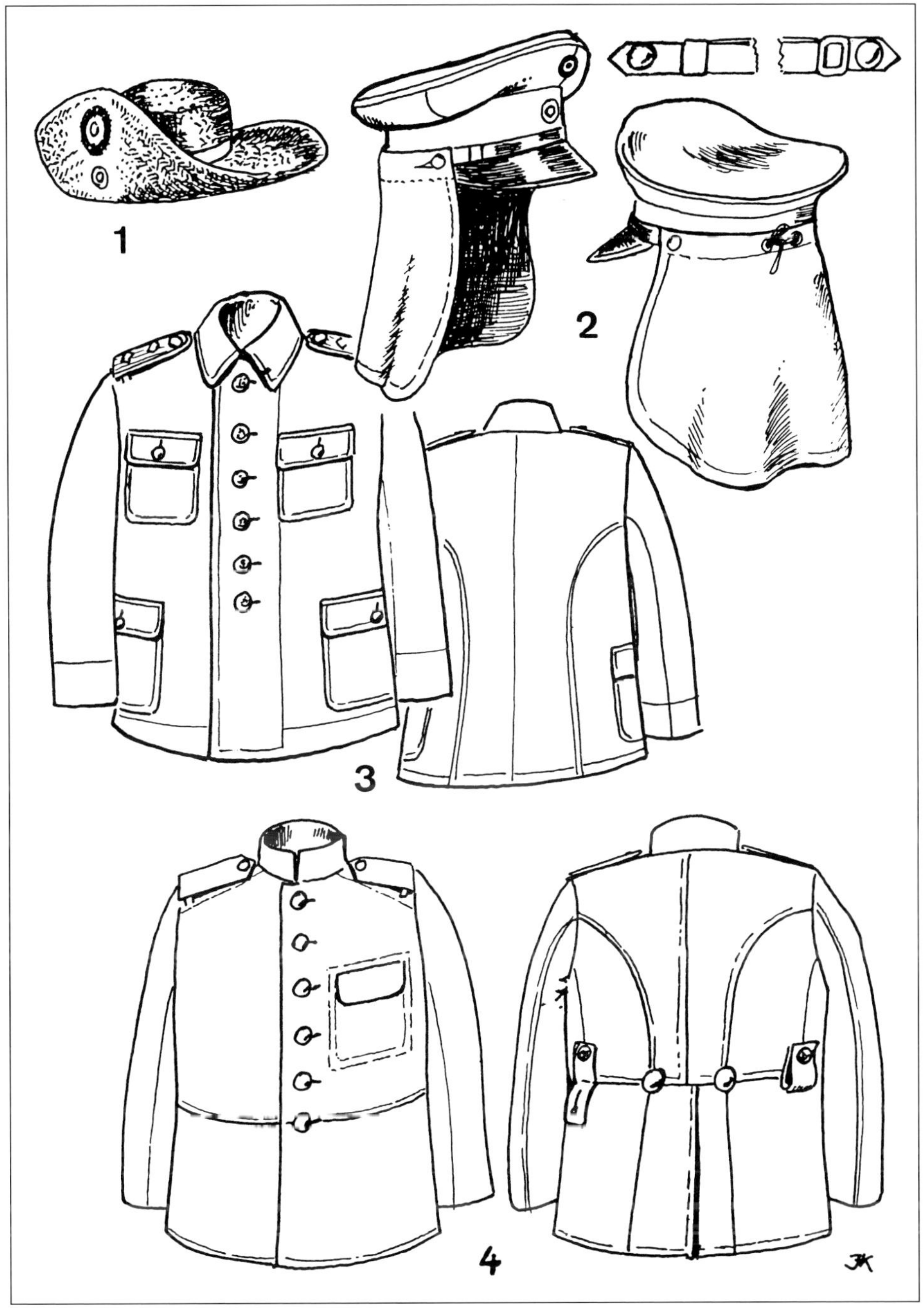

Tafel C. Illustrates the summer uniform, M1900, the summer feldmützen for both men and officers, and five detailed views of the blouse (rockbluse).

Headgear for tropical use, tropical blouse for officers, and khaki drill blouse for enlisted personnel.

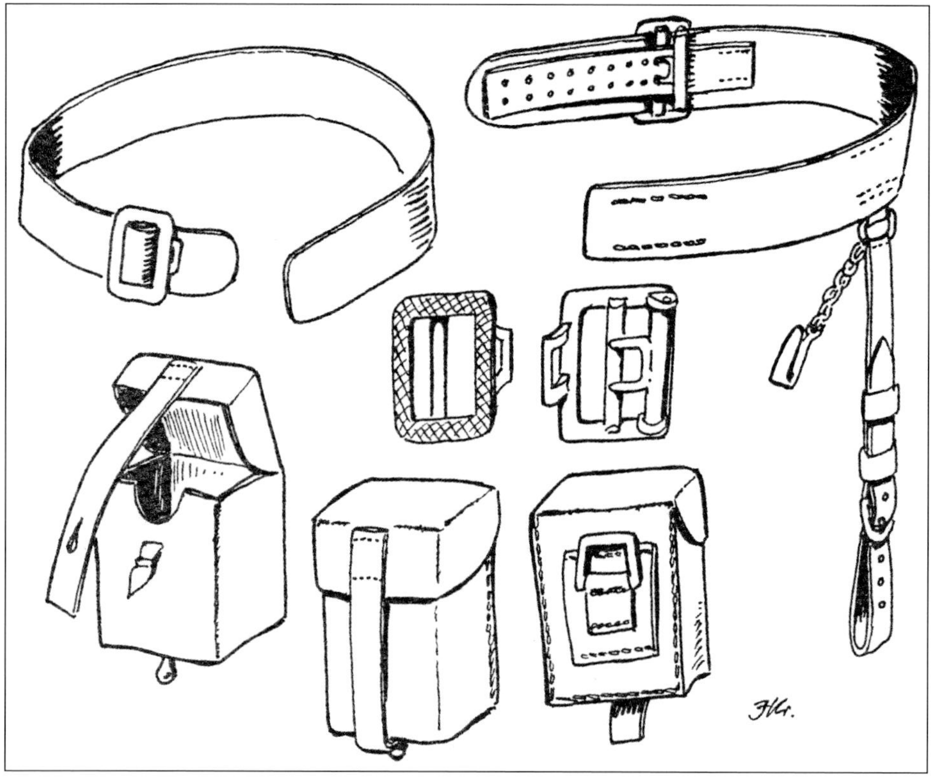

Brown leather waistbelt, sword belt, buckles and cartridge boxes as issued to the Expedition Korps.

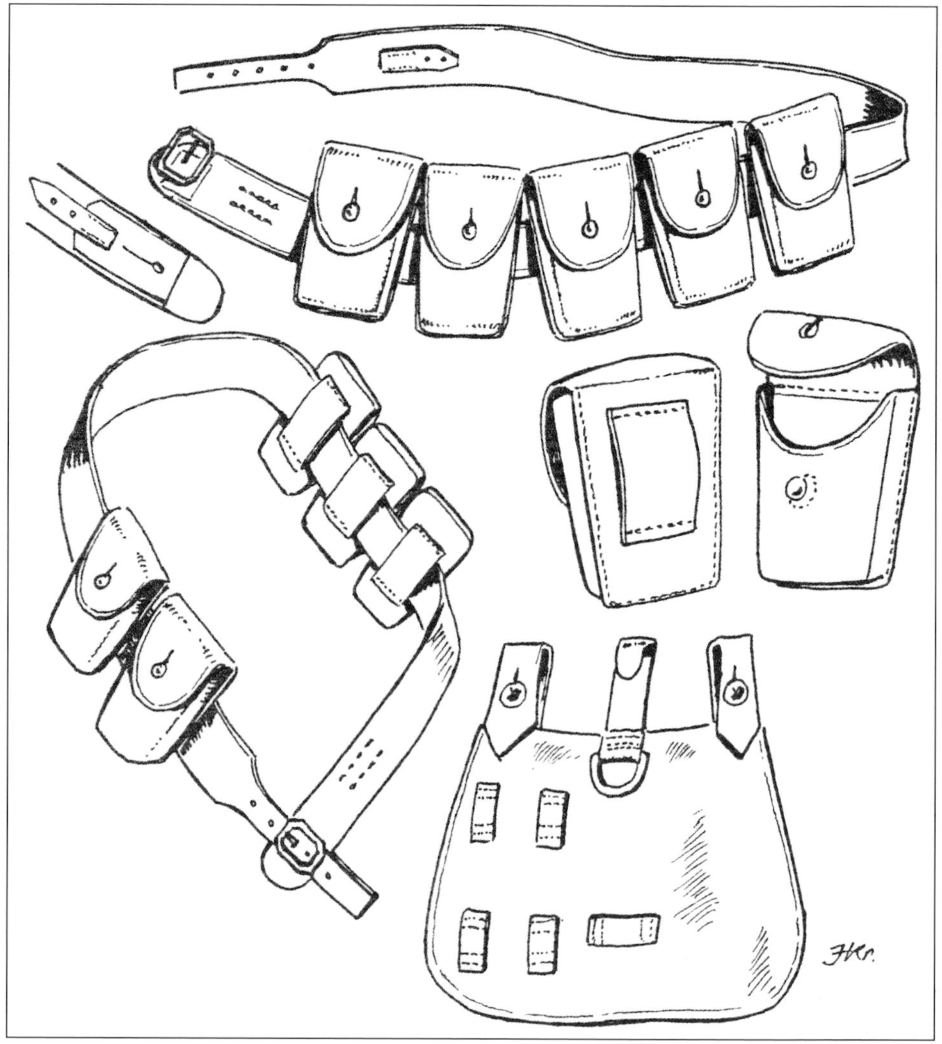

Leather bandolier, cartridge boxes and breadbag as issued to the mounted troops. Note the differences between the cartridge boxes of the mounted troops and infantry.

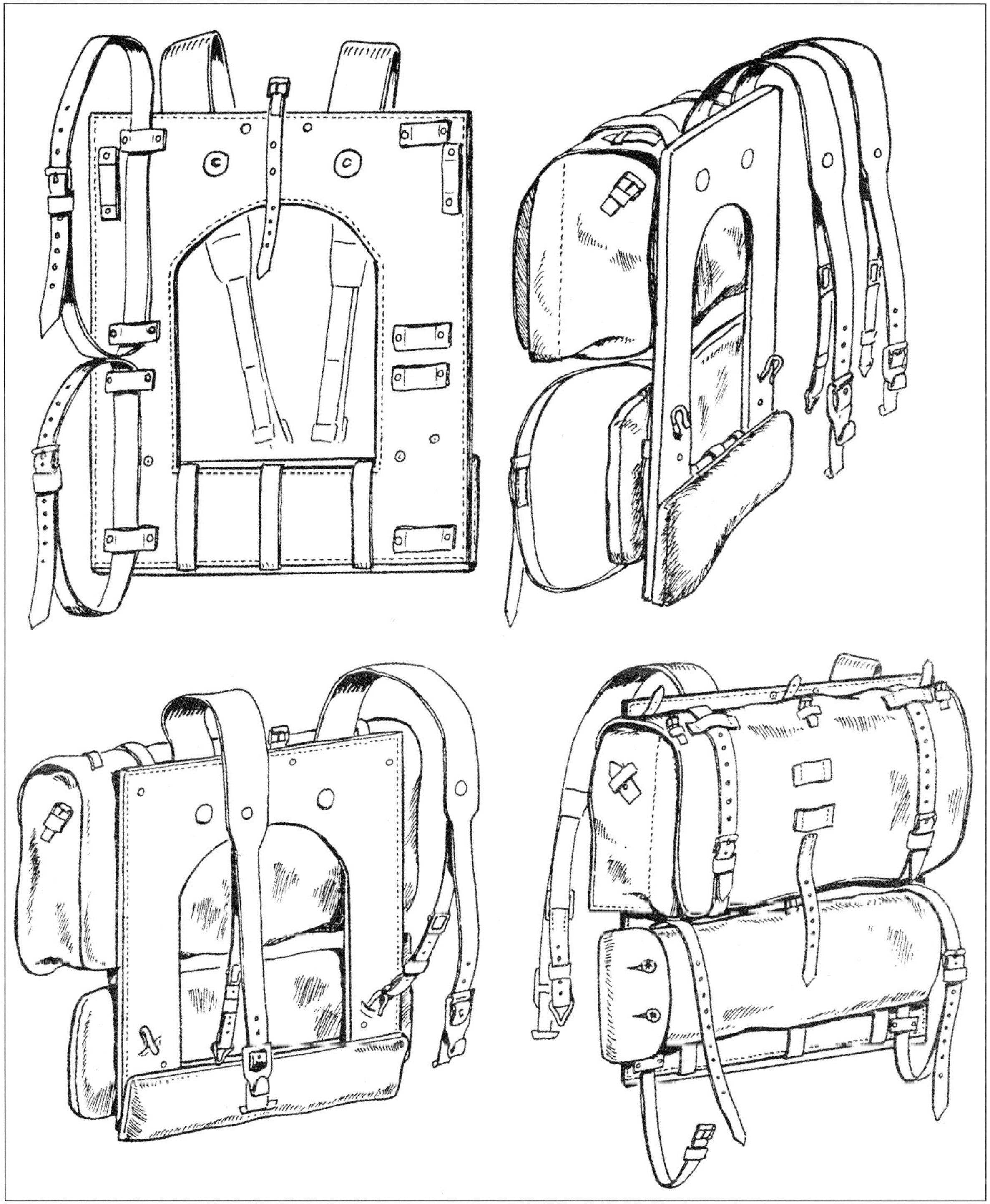

Rucksack (rückengestells) carrying board shown empty, with the Gepäcksack and Zeltzubehörbeutel (Zeltbahn accessories) attached.

CHAPTER SIX

Artist's Drawings and Paintings

The imagination of military artists of the late 19th and early 20th centuries was stirred by various physical encounters in Germany's new colonies, the creation of the Schutztruppe, and the resulting punitive expeditions against the natives in Africa. Writers chronicled these events in book and periodical form which then called for illustrations. There was a demand for black and white and colored action pictures and depictions of the varied uniforms of the Schutztruppen and Naval forces. A *Who's Who* of popular military artists worked in this genre.

Carl Becker, born in 1862, studied at the Karlsruhe Akademie, and became professionally active in Berlin, later operating from a studio in Munich. His early oil paintings of the Franco-Prussian War cavalry actions were highly acclaimed and he later illustrated many military books, including *Deutsche Reiter in Südwest* by Friedrich Freiheer von Dincklage-Campe. Some of Becker's illustrations are included in this section.

Erich R. Döbrich, born in 1896, later resided and worked in the area of Berlin-Steglitz, signing many of his paintings "Döbrich-Steglitz". He was particularly active during the early 1930s, depicting the blossoming of the new German armed forces at that time. His active military service began in 1939, and Army Lists show him as a reserve Oberleutnant and later Rittmeister d.Rz.V. assigned to the "Propaganda-Ersatz-Abteilung, Potsdam". In 1945, during the defense of Berlin against the Russians, Döbrich commanded the "Handwerken der Kommandantur Berlin", a last-ditch unit made up of artists and craftsman. After the fall of Berlin he was listed as "missing" and his body was never found. Five of Döbrich's "Schutztruppen" paintings shown here illustrate his skill and diversity of subject matter.

Ernst Zimmer, 1864-1924, studied in Danzig and was a master student of Louis Braun in Munich. Zimmer specialized in military scenes, working in oils, watercolors, and pen and ink. His pen and ink work was featured in C. Tanera's *Deutschland's Kämpfe in Ost-Asien 1900-1901* which covered the Boxer Rebellion and is included in this section.

Further examples included are the work of Richard Knötel, 1857-1914, Anton Hoffmann of Munich, C.W. Allers from his *Alltag in der Kaiserlichen Marine um 1890*, Ludwig Scharf, soldier artist, Englishmen R.S. Marrion and Gary Embleton, and German military artist Paul Pietsch. Pietsch (1879-1973), was active, as was Knötel, in portraying German uniforms of all periods. Pietsch's style varied over the years, but his attention to detail never faltered. His groundbreaking work *Formations- und Uniformierungsgeschichte des preussischen Heeres*, first published in 1912, was later republished in the 1970s and is one of the finest on the subject. The Pietsch color illustrations of Marine-Infanterie and See-Bataillon subjects are from original illustrations held by the Anne S.K. Brown Military Collection, Brown University, Providence, Rhode Island.

Carl Becker

Becker's cover illustration for the book Deutsche Reiter in Südwest.

The Kaiser inspected the Schutztruppe in Potsdam prior to their departure for Deutsch-Südwestafrika, 15 June 1894.

On the morning of 18 January 1904 Oberleutnant Bolfmann led the charge with twelve men in a furious engagement against the Hereros.

On 4 February 1904 Hauptmann Franke led a charge against the Hereros near the town of Omaruru.

Major von Estorff and Hauptmann Franke led a charge against the Hereros near Otjibiamaparero on 25 February 1904.

Trompeter Lehmann led the mounted relief of "1. Marine-Infanterie-Kompagnie" pinned down by the Hereros near Okaharui on 3 April 1904. The Marines lost the engagement with twenty-eight killed and eight wounded.

The 5. Batterie of Artillery in action near Hamakari on 11 August 1904.

Mounted troops and artillery in an engagement by "Gross-Nabas" on 3 January 1905.

Surprise attack on a wagon train by the Hereros on 20 July 1905. Two protecting cavalrymen courageously paid with their blood.

Rapid firing guns in action near Hartebeestmund on 24 October 1905.

Hauptmann Bech led his men against the Hottentots at Ban Rooisvlen on 4 May 1906.

A patrol of camel riders pursue the Hottentots over the desert wastes of the Kalahari on 16 March 1908.

Erich Döbrich

Two artillery batteries in action with the Gebirgskannone L/17 of 1908. These guns were developed at Rheinmetall and twelve of these guns formed three batteries of the Schutztruppen in Ostafrika.

Mounted Askaris wearing the red fez of Kamerun troops as well as the red collars and insignia of that colony's uniform. A German officer seen in the background leads them. Note the black, white and red lance pennons.

German officers and Askaris in a charge against the British in Ostafrica. A native standard bearer closely follows the officer, sword drawn, leading the advance. The period would have been later in the War as the Askaris are armed with Gew.98s firing smokeless powder.

A mounted patrol of Schutztruppen cross a desert area. An officer in the lead, followed by an NCO and five troopers, make up the strength of this unit.

Döbrich captures the dry heat of the Kalahari Desert in this painting of the camel riders of Deutsch-Südwestafrika. The riders in cornflower blue-trimmed uniforms carry whips to urge the camels to a faster gait when necessary.

Ernst Zimmer

This Zimmer illustration of a Naval landing party was embossed on the cover of Tanera's book Deutschlands Kämpfe in Ost-Asien 1900-1901.

The first Naval landing detachment celebrates its arrival in China. Note the salute to the National flag of Germany, not the military or Naval-style ensign.

Besetzung des Pagodenhügels.

A gun crew struggles to move their six pound, 9 cm C/73 field gun and limber into position on a hillside near a Chinese pagoda.

Boxer.

A typical Boxer as encountered during the Rebellion.

Chineſe der deutſchen berittenen Marineartillerie in Kiautſchou.

A Chinese attached to the German mounted Marine Artillery.

Deutſcher berittener Marineartilleriſt in Kiautſchou.

A German mounted crewman of the Marine Artillery.

A typical sailor, part of the Marine Brigade at Tsingtau, China.

China, 1900. A Naval landing party sailor stands guard over a light Naval field cannon.

German Naval officers aboard a steam launch survey the harbor fortifications near Tsingtau, China.

Graf Waldersee, commanding German forces in China.

A mounted See-Soldieriere about to capture a fleeing Chinese.

Anton Hoffmann

Anton Hoffmann, the versatile Bavarian military artist, illustrates mounted Schutztruppen in a dismounted engagement, Ostafrica, 1915.

Richard Knötel

Knötel (1857-1914) painted this illustration as part of his contribution to the uniform book Königlich prussische Armee 1905. The East Asiatic Occupation Brigade and Schutztruppen are identified as follows: (1) Marine-Feld-Batterie, mounted; (2) Train Soldier; (3) Infantryman in field marching uniform; (4) Pionier, summer uniform; (5) Mounted Artillery Officer; (6) Infantry standard bearer, East Asian Infantry Regiments 1-6. Standard presented in 1900; (7) Cavalryman in overcoat and field uniform, Deutsch-Südwestafrika; (8) Mounted Schutztruppe officer in service dress, Deutsch-Südwestafrika; (9) Cavalryman in tropical dress (tropenuniform), Deutsch-Südwestafrika; (10) Officer parade dress (Kamerun and Togo); (11) Mounted cavalryman, field service uniform; (12) NCO, white parade dress (Kamerun and Togo); (13) Sergeant in Home Service uniform (Ostafrica); (14) NCO in greatcoat (Ostafrica); (15) Sudanese Askari.

Krickel and Lange

Krickel and Lange were responsible for a classic study of the uniforms of the Prussian army, as well as the Bavarians and other German states. The artist Krickel also illustrated other uniform studies and this is an example of his work entitled Marine und Schutztruppen in den Tropen. This illustration includes Schutztruppen and Askaris from the African colonies including Naval forces in target practice. Interesting is the revolving cannon depicted in the lower right view.

Ludwig Scharf

Scharf's unique style is shown in this illustration of a mounted cavalryman. Among the mounted troops was a small volunteer band of South African Boers known as the Vrij Korps led by Andries de Wet. Note that the kokarde is not red, white, and black which indicates Scharf's intent to show one of these volunteers or "Sudafrickanischen Freikorps" members.

Christian Wilhelm Allers

Allers' pen and ink drawing titled In den Tropen depicts Oberbootsmannsmat Heinrich Westphal from the ship S.M.S. Elisabeth off the East African coast. He is in the landing uniform complete with an 1885 tropenhelm with a large neck protector. From Alltag in der Kaiserlichen Marine um 1890.

Allers' drawing shows a sailor in landing rig from the ship S.M.S. Niobe.

Allers captures that certain look of nobility in his portrait of Leutnant zur See, later Korvettenkapitän, Freiherr von Erhardt in tropical uniform off Samoa, 1888.

Gary Embleton and R.J. Marrion

These two talented artists teamed up to illustrate a series of articles which appeared in the no longer published Tradition magazine. Embleton's drawing is of a camel detachment rider whose hat and uniform are trimmed in cornflower blue. The leather equipment and camel harness are brown.

Vize-Feldwebel, Fahnentrager (standard bearer) by Ron Marrion after a photograph. The gorget and chains are white metal; the Fahnentrager badge bears crossed flags, an Imperial crown and cipher in yellow on a sand grey background. The jacket collar is trimmed with silver braid and silver NCO rank buttons. The trousers are sand grey cord material and the jacket is khaki drill.

CHAPTER SEVEN

Kaiserliche Marine - Ost-Asian

Wilhelm II, soon after becoming Kaiser, recognized the need to increase and update his obsolete Naval forces. The modernization was not only to compete with British Naval strength, but also to protect and supply his growing German overseas colonies. In 1898 a bill was passed by the Reichstag calling for the immediate new construction of a powerful German fleet. Wilhelm II took a deep personal interest in his Navy, exercising its control by placing his brother, Prince Henry, as its nominal head. At the turn of the 20th century, in the waters of Eastern Asia, the German Naval fleet consisted of 4 Grosser Kreuzer (heavy cruisers), 7 Kliener Kreuzer (light cruisers), and 4 Kannenboot (gunboats), 4 Linienschiffen (transport liners), and 3 Doppelschrauber-Torpedoboote (twin-screw torpedo boats).

The uniforms worn by the shipboard personnel were the traditional navy blue for all levels. Officers, when on tropical duty and in extremely warm weather, wore high-collared white cotton uniforms, and if an officer was serving on land, a tan tropical uniform of the same cut as the white jacket was approved, but with a stand and fall collar. Enlisted men wore white cotton uniforms under the same conditions.

The following eight captioned Naval plates are taken from the Unsere Truppen in Ost-Asien, published by Verlag von Moritz Ruhl in Leipzig. In the same volume Ruhl illustrated the uniforms of "Das Armee-Oberkommando in Ost-Asien" which was under the command of Generalfeldmarschall Graf Waldersee and are included in the Ostasiatischen Expedition section of this work.

Korvettenkapitän. im Jacket. **Fregattenkapitän.** Dienstanzug. **Kapitänleutnant.** Grosse Uniform. **Vizeadmiral.** Grosse Uniform. **Oberleutnant z. See.** im Ueberzieher. **Leutnant z. See.** Tropen-Anzug.

Marine-Infanterie.

Unteroffizier. Dienst-Anzug. — Hornist. Paradeanzug. — Oberleutnant. im Ueberrock. — Stabsoffizier. Paradeanzug. — Zeug-Kapitänleutnant. Grosser Dienstanzug. — Torpeder-Leutnant. Dienstanzug. — Feuerwerks-Oberleutnant. Tagesanzug.

Ober-Lootse.
Tagesanzug.

Torpedo-
Oberingenieur.
Tagesanzug.

Marine-
Stabsingenieur,
Grosse Uniform.

Marine-
Assistenzarzt.
Tagesanzug.

Marine-
Oberstabsarzt I. Cl.

Marine-
Baurath.

Grosser Dienstanzug.

Marine-
Bauführer
im Jacket.

Stabszahlmeister. Tagesanzug. — Zahlmeister. Grosse Uniform. — Marine-Intendanturrath. Grosse Uniform. — Marine-Auditeur. Grosse Uniform. — Garnisonbau-Oberingenieur. Grosse Uniform. — Garnisonbau-Assistent. Dienstanzug.

Marine-Apotheker.
Tagesanzug.

Baupersonal d. Werften
u. d. Torpedowesens.

Bauinspecter.
Tagesanzug.

Oberbaurath.
Grosse Uniform.

Betriebs- und Verwaltungspersonal d. Werften.

Oberbootsmann.
Tagesanzug.

Betriebssekretär. Rendant.
Tagesanzug.

Deckoffiziere.
Ober-Bootsmann.
Maschinist.
Musikdirigent
Stabshoboist.
Seekade'
Fähnrich z. See.

Matrosen-Divisonen.

Feldwebel.	Hoboist.	Ober-Steuermannsmaat.	Ober-Matrose.	Matrosen.	
Paradeanzug.	Paradeanzug.	Sontagsanzug.	Ordonnanzanzug.	Wachtanzug.	im weissen Hemd.

Werft-Divisonen.

Heizer. Ordonnanzanzug.

Ober-Feuermeisters-Maat. Paradeanzug.

Feldwebel. im Jacket.

Maschinisten-Maat. im Ueberzieher.

Schiffsjunge.

Ober-Matrose. Tropen-Anzug.

The numbered figures 1-8 in this illustration by R. Knötel depict the naval uniforms of officers and enlisted men and in number 9, the Marine-Infanterie. Figures 10-14 show the "Schutztruppe in Ostafrika".

CHAPTER EIGHT

Marine Infanterie and III. See-Bataillon

The Marine-Infanterie was the elite force of Naval personnel created to defend by land harbors and military installations and also acted as a Naval police force maintaining order among the sailors of the fleet. They were a highly effective offensive landing force. When army units were unavailable, the Marine-Infanterie took the place of the regular army in the colonies and other German territories. There were three Bataillons in the force, but the III. See-Bataillon was the one most involved, particularly in China at Kiautschou and Tsingtau.

The III. See-Bataillon consisted of the following: four companies, one Chinese company, one Marine-Feldbatterie, and the Matrosen-Artillerie-Detachement at Kiautschou. The Chinese company was commanded by two Oberleutnants. The four regular companies were led by four Hauptmanns assisted by five Oberleutnants and seven Leutnants. The Marine-Feldbatterie was led by a Hauptmann and two Leutnants, while the Matrosen-Artillerie-Detachement Kiautschou was led by a Naval Kapitäleutnant.

The Marine-Infanterie, by the nature of its varied duties, required a variety of uniforms. The Home Service uniform, or peace-time uniform, was dark blue and cut in the Army pattern. The uniform collar and cuffs were white with Litzen applied in the Garde Regiment style. The shoulder straps were also white with yellow crossed anchors, Imperial Crown over a banner and the Bataillon roman numeral number below the crossed anchors. The uniform was piped in white down the front, around the cuffs and rear coat flaps.

Officer's tunics were identical in cut to the enlisted men and NCOs, but made of finer quality material with insignia of gold bullion thread. Visored caps were worn by officers and NCOs, while the enlisted ranks wore a visorless mütze similar to the Army model. The tschako was worn on shipboard and field service duty, while the tropenhelm was worn in tropical service on land. Both officers and the enlisted ranks stationed in China and other Pacific duty stations in hot weather wore a khaki field uniform of the Army cut as seen in the following illustrations. To add to the many variations of uniforms worn by the Marine-Infanterie was the blue or grey Litewka worn in cooler weather, the regular, or standard, Fleet sailor's jumper, and bellbottoms in blue or white restricted to sea duty, and for the mounted 5. Kompanie III. See-Bataillon, a grey-green Litewka and field cap cover worn with blue riding breeches and leather strapped leggings.

Marine-Infanterie and Officials. Verlag von Max Hochsprung, Berlin.

Marine Field Service, Parade and Musicians Uniforms. Militär-Informations-Postkarten, No.24. Carl Henckel, Pirma.

Unteroffizier vom III. Seebataillon
in Tsingtau (Kiautschou) von der Marine-Feld-Batterie, um 1913. Aquarell von E. Döbrich

NCO, III. See-Bataillon, Marine Field Battery, 1913, Tsingtau. E. Döbrich, Das Ehrenklied das Soldaten, Martin Lezius.

Marine-Infanterie, Home and Abroad. Militär Information-Tafeln. Carl Henckel, Pirma.

III. See-Bataillon Brown Uniforms. Pietsch. Marineinfanterie und Schutztruppen. Major Eberhard Hettler.

III. See-Bataillon 5. (Mounted) Company. Pietsch.

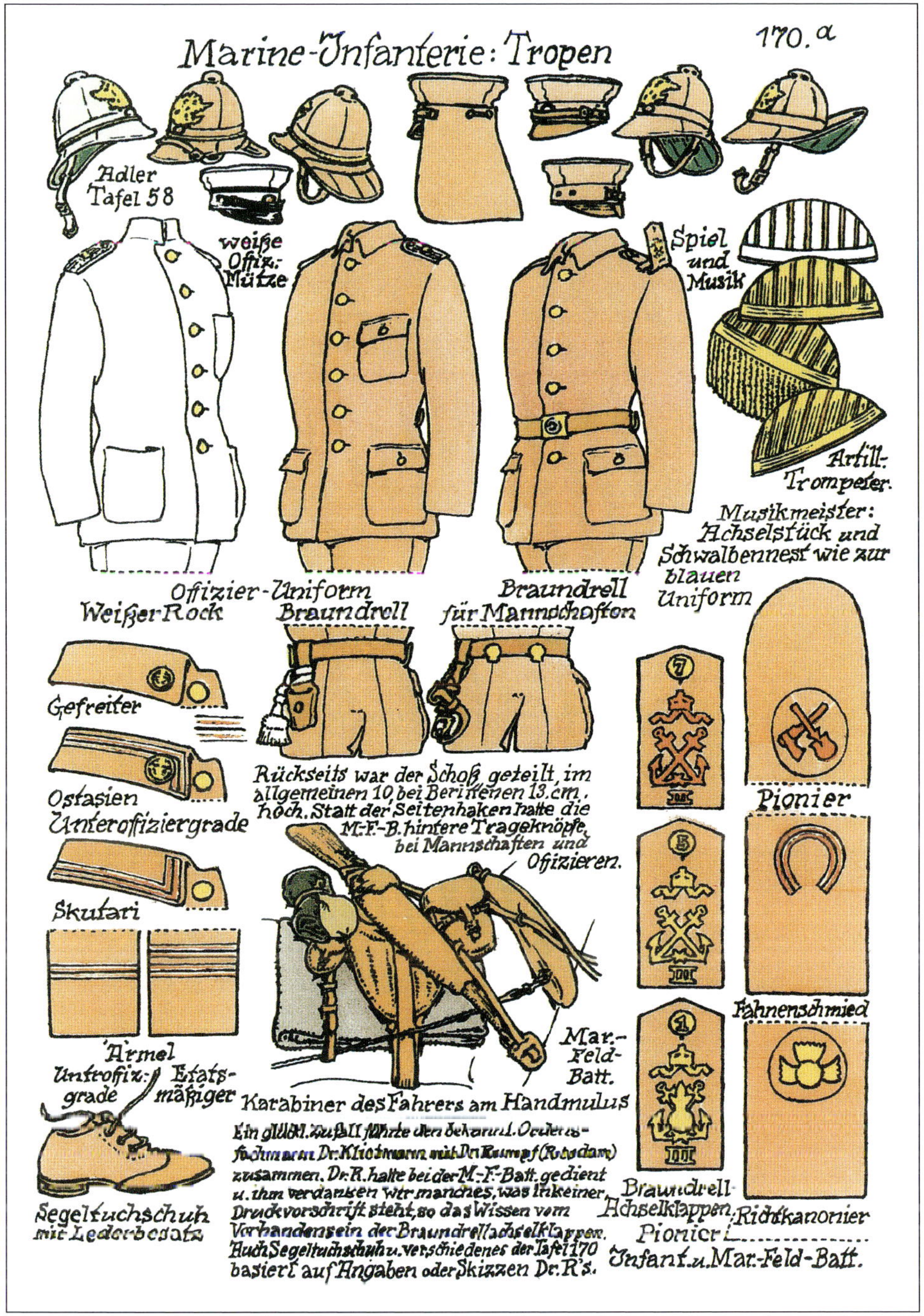

Marine Infanterie Tropical Uniforms. Pietsch. Uniformenkunde Das Deutsches Heer. Knotel, Pietsch, and Collas. second edition, W. Spemann, Stuttgart, 1982.

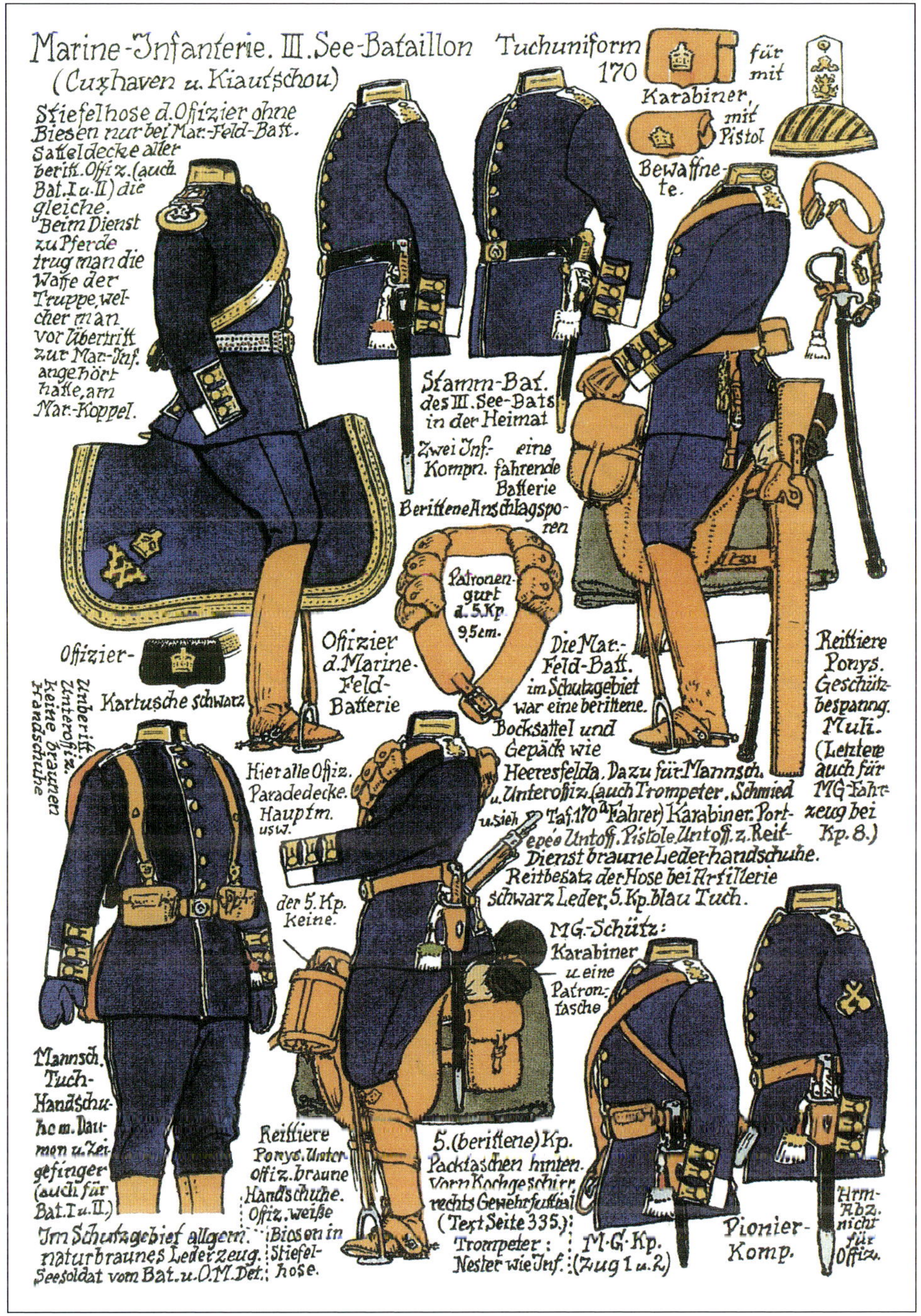

MarineInfanterie Cloth (wool) Uniforms. Pietsch. Uniformenkunde Das Deutsches Heer. Knotel, Pietsch, and Collas. second edition, W. Spemann, Stuttgart, 1982.

See-Bataillon Dress Uniforms and Insignia. Pietsch. Uniformenkunde Das Deutsches Heer. Knötel, Pietsch, and Collas. second edition, W. Spemann, Stuttgart, 1982.

Staff Officer, Marine Infanterie. Parade Dress. Uniformen der Marine und Schutztruppen. Waldorf Astoria.

Captain, Marine Infanterie, Uberoch, Paletot. Uniformen der Marine und Schutztruppen. Waldorf Astoria.

1st Leutnant, Marine Infanterie. Formal Mess Dress. Uniformen der Marine und Schutztruppen. Waldorf Astoria.

Leutnant, Marine Infanterie. Tropical Uniform. Uniformen der Marine und Schutztruppen. Waldorf Astoria.

Captain, Marine Field Battery. Brown Drill Service Dress. Uniformen der Marine und Schutztruppen. Waldorf Astoria.

Feldwebel, See Bataillon. Parade Dress. Uniformen der Marine und Schutztruppen. Waldorf Astoria.

Seesoldat, II. See-Bataillon. Field Service Dress. Uniformen der Marine und Schutztruppen. Waldorf Astoria.

Mounted Seesoldat, 5. Komp. III. See-Bataillon, in Litewka. Uniformen der Marine und Schutztruppen. Waldorf Astoria.

Sergeant, Pionier-Kompagnie, III. See-Bataillon. Service Dress. Uniformen der Marine und Schutztruppen. Waldorf Astoria.

Driver, Marine-Feldbatterie. Brown Drill Tunic. Uniformen der Marine und Schutztruppen. Waldorf Astoria.

Non-commissioned Officer, III. Stamm-See-Bataillon. Mantel. Uniformen der Marine und Schutztruppen. Waldorf Astoria.

Polizeitruppe, New Guinea, Kaiser Wilhelm's Land. Soldier in Field Marching Order. Uniformen der Marine und Schutztruppen. Waldorf Astoria.

Polizeitruppe, Jap (Yap) Polizeisoldat in Parade Uniform. Uniformen der Marine und Schutztruppen. Waldorf Astoria.

Fita-Fita Samoa. Governor's Orderly. Uniformen der Marine und Schutztruppen. Waldorf Astoria.

Paul Pietsch created the following unpublished illustrations of one of his favorite subjects, the III. See-Bataillon Imperial Marines. The original illustrations are in the Anne S.K. Brown Military Collection, Brown University, Providence, RI. Pietsch carefully captioned the illustrations which appear here in the original German, and need no translation.

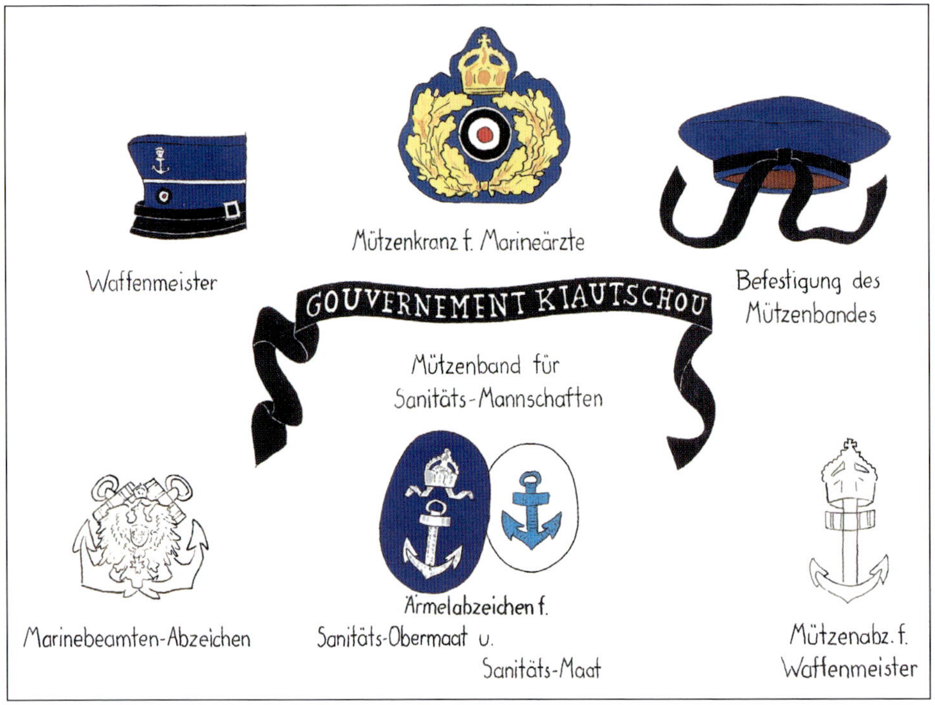
Mützenkranz f. Marineärzte
Waffenmeister
Befestigung des Mützenbandes
GOUVERNEMENT KIAUTSCHOU
Mützenband für Sanitäts-Mannschaften
Marinebeamten-Abzeichen
Ärmelabzeichen f. Sanitäts-Obermaat u. Sanitäts-Maat
Mützenabz. f. Waffenmeister

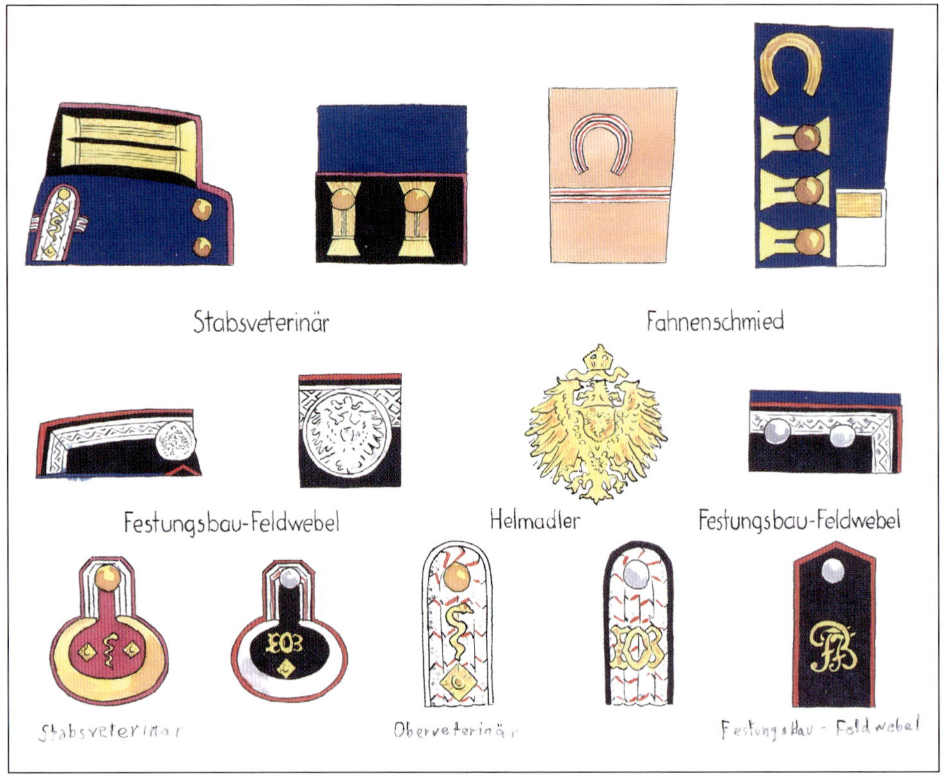
Stabsveterinär
Fahnenschmied
Festungsbau-Feldwebel
Helmadler
Festungsbau-Feldwebel
Stabsveterinär
Oberveterinär
Festungsbau-Feldwebel

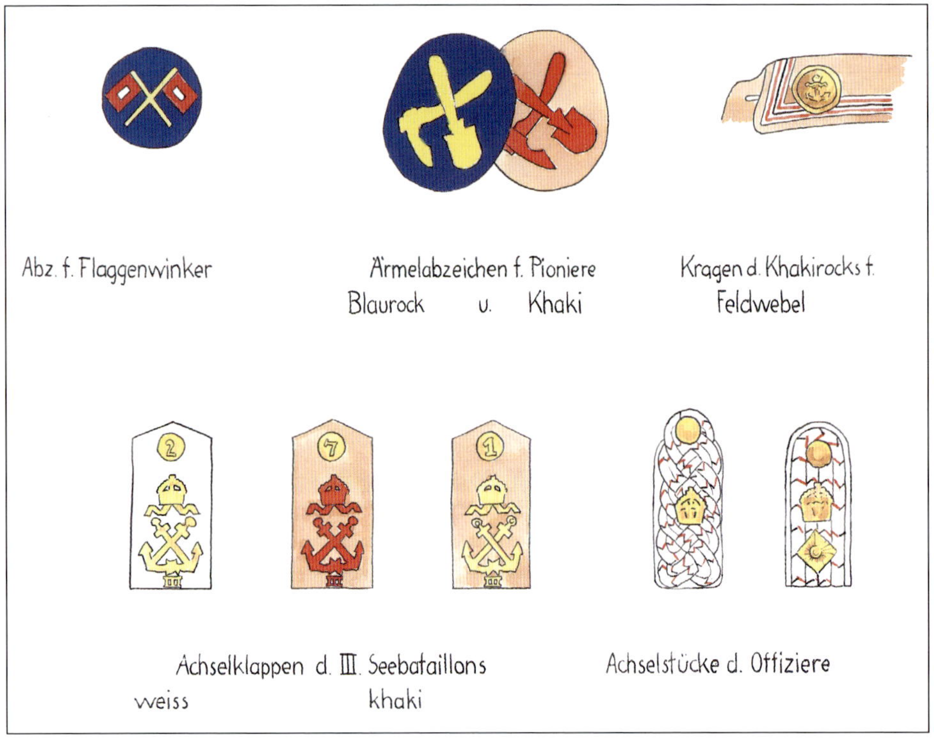
Abz. f. Flaggenwinker
Ärmelabzeichen f. Pioniere Blaurock u. Khaki
Kragen d. Khakirocks f. Feldwebel
Achselklappen d. III. Seebataillons weiss khaki
Achselstücke d. Offiziere

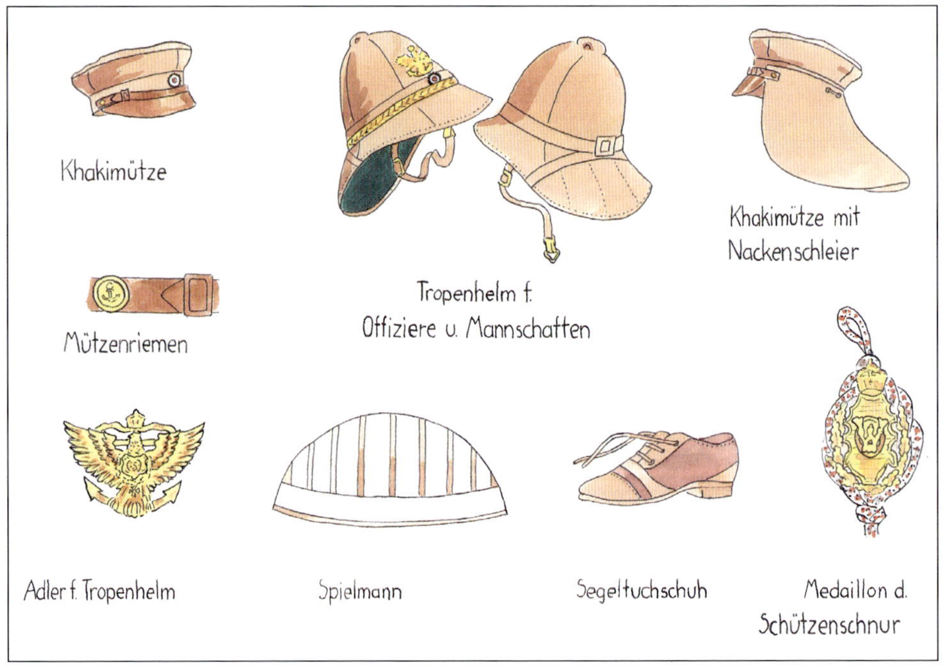
Khakimütze
Khakimütze mit Nackenschleier
Mützenriemen
Tropenhelm f. Offiziere u. Mannschaften
Adler f. Tropenhelm
Spielmann
Segeltuchschuh
Medaillon d. Schützenschnur

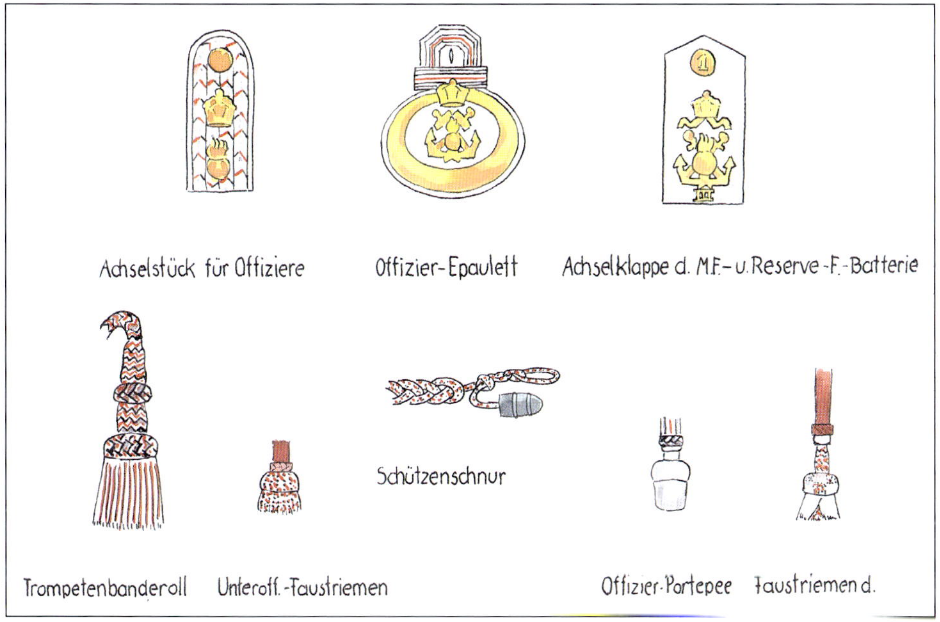
Achselstück für Offiziere
Offizier-Epaulett
Achselklappe d. M.F.- u. Reserve-F.-Batterie
Trompetenbanderoll
Unteroff.-Faustriemen
Schützenschnur
Offizier-Portepee
Faustriemen d.

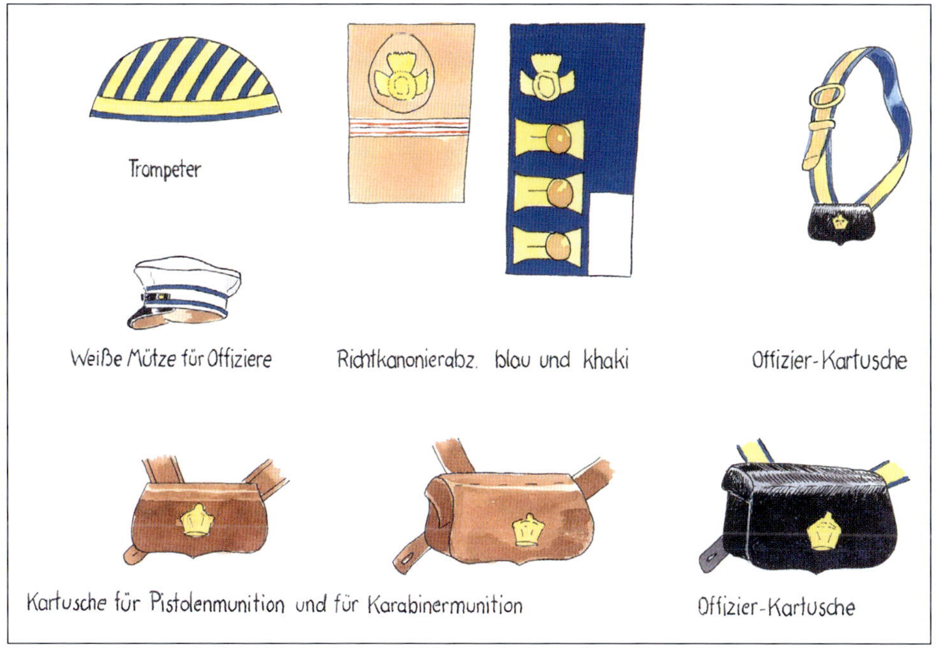
Trompeter
Weiße Mütze für Offiziere
Richtkanonierabz. blau und khaki
Offizier-Kartusche
Kartusche für Pistolenmunition und für Karabinermunition
Offizier-Kartusche

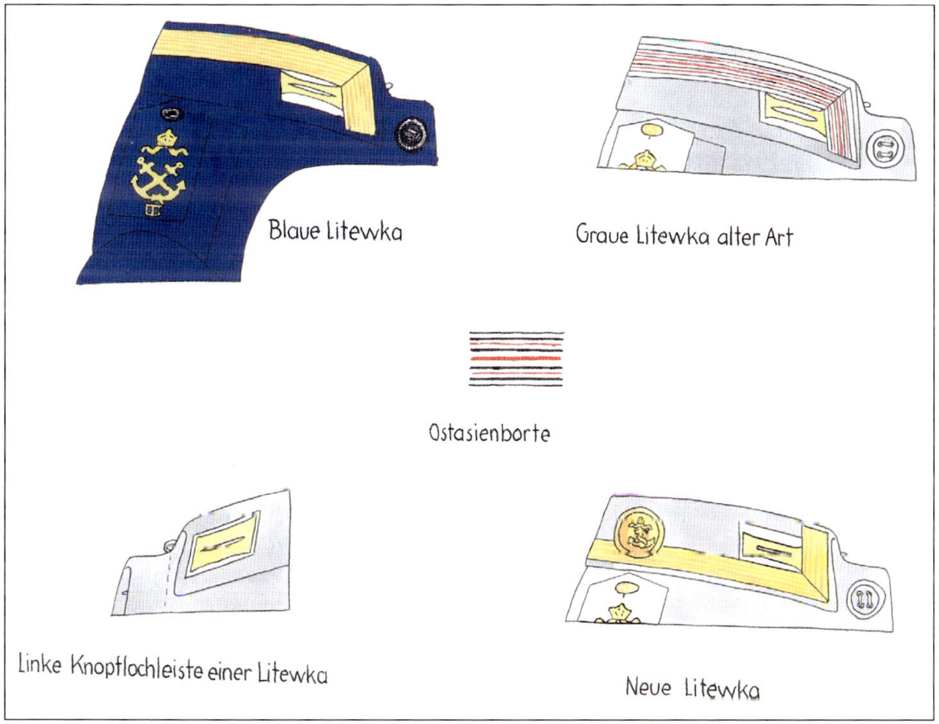
Blaue Litewka
Graue Litewka alter Art
Ostasienborte
Linke Knopflochleiste einer Litewka
Neue Litewka

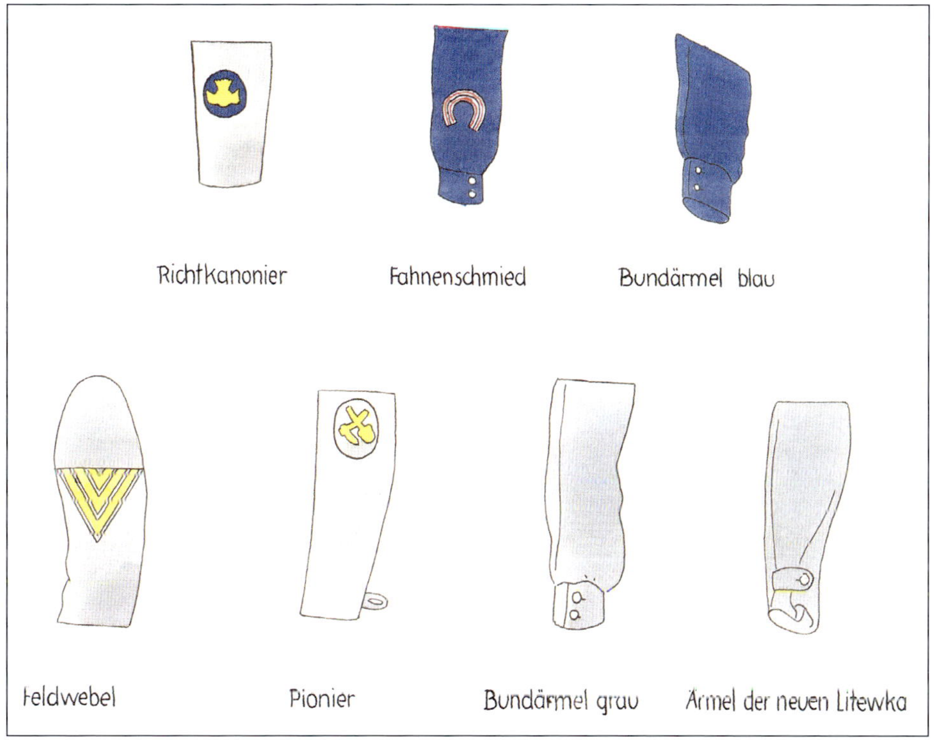
Richtkanonier
Fahnenschmied
Bundärmel blau
Feldwebel
Pionier
Bundärmel grau
Ärmel der neuen Litewka

Oberzahlmeister

Waffenmeister

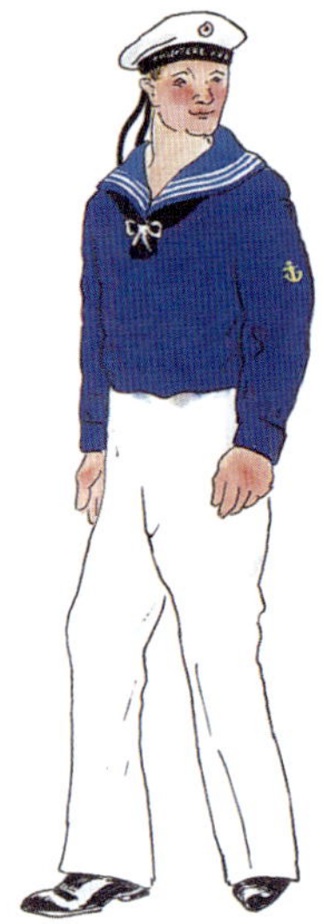

Sanitätsmaat im blauen Hemd

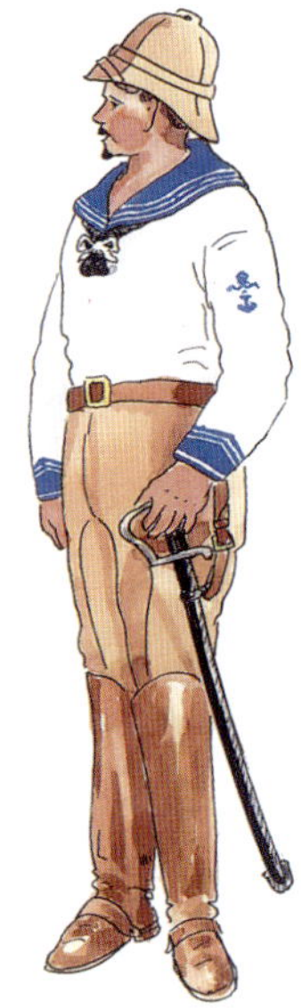

Sanitäts-Obermaat

Offizier-Litewka

Veterinär-Offizier zur Parade

Festungsbau-Offizier in weißer Uniform

Weiße Uniform für Offiziere

Stabsarzt im weißen Rock

Feldwebel der Pionierkomp.

Seesoldat

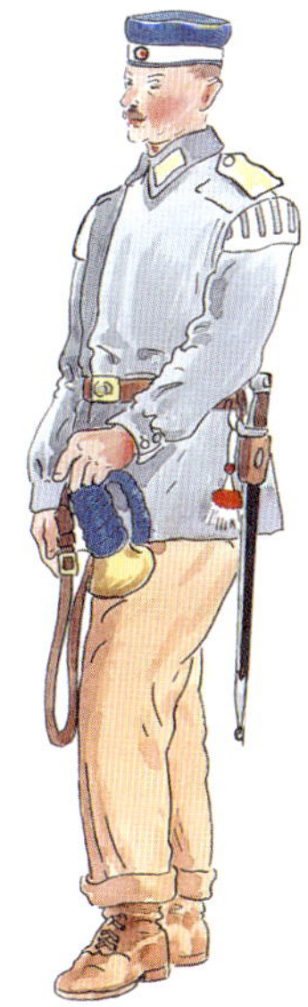
Hornist

Blauhemd

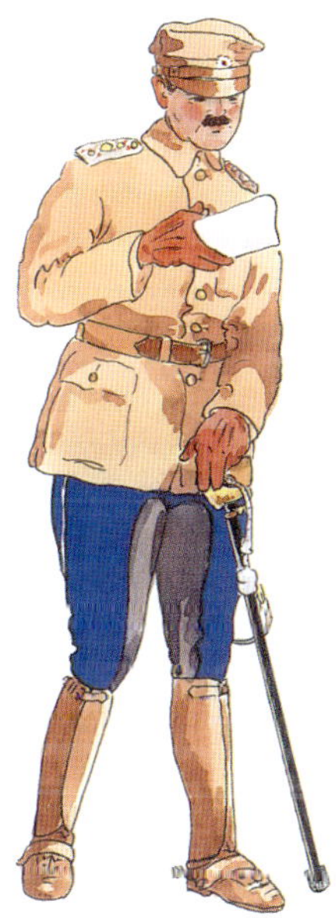
Offizier

Gefreiter

Kanonier der Reserve Feld Batterie

Trompeter

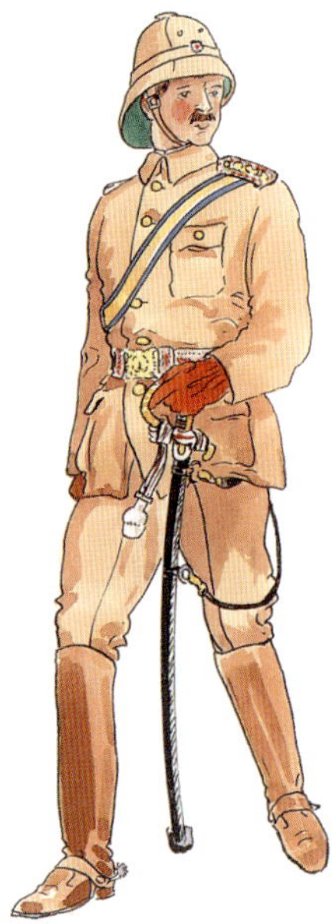

Offizier

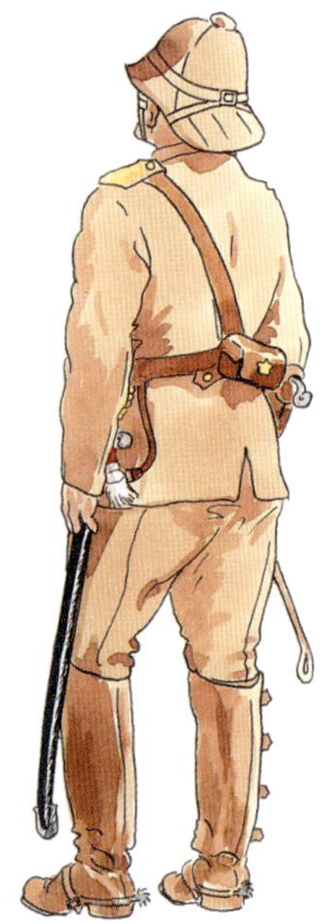

Fahrer

Schütze der M.G.-Züge

Pionier (7. Komp)

Etatsmäßiger Feldwebel (Lehr-Batl.)

Fahenschmied

Veterinäroffizier in khaki

Gefreiter (Kapitulant)

Marine-Feld-Batterie

Trompeter

5. (berittene) Komp. des III. Seebataillons

5. (berittene) Komp. des III. See-Bataillons

Trompeter

Landsturmmann

Khaki-Uniform

Khaki-Uniform

Wachmann in grauer Uniform

Ölrock

Grauer Mantel

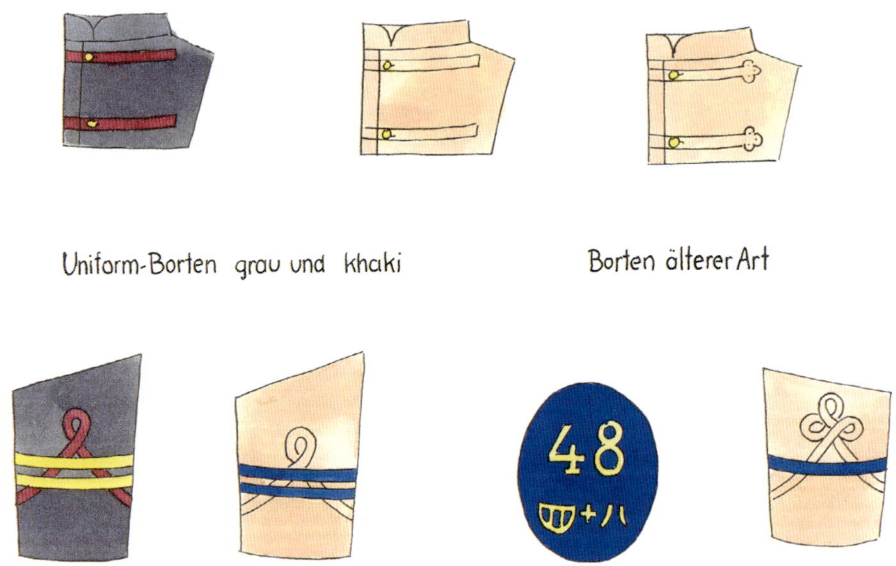

Uniform-Borten grau und khaki

Borten älterer Art

Ärmelborten grau und khaki

Ärmelabzeichen

Borten älterer Art

Photo Section: Marine-Infanterie and III. See-Bataillon

In 1907 Heinrich Wagener, at the age of eighteen, joined the German Imperial Marines and was attached to the III. See-Bataillon. He served with them in a machine gun company until 1910. Much of Wagener's service was spent in Tsingtau, China, the site of the largest Imperial German Naval base outside of Germany. The Marines were there to protect the base from land assault, which came in 1914 from Japanese forces. Tsingtau quickly fell to the superior Japanese forces.

While in China, Wagener arranged for the creation of a quality photo album depicting areas of local interest and his unit's activities while there. The original album is bound in decorated red lacquer covers (8"x10"); the front surmounted with a beautifully executed Chinese dragon, cut and engraved in mother-of-pearl. The album contains ninety professionally taken photographs mounted two per page. The subject matter varies from the Marines arrival in Tsingtau to maneuvers, camp and barrack scenes, the Kaiser's birthday in 1909, views of the harbor and ships to rather grizzly stock photos of Chinese criminals and beheadings. Those photographs considered of greater interest are included, and are captioned in the original German or loosely translated. The photographs appear in the order found in the album.

Heinrich Wagener's arrival in Tsingtau, China.

III. See Bataillon upon arrival, marching up Friedrichstrasse.

Friedrichstrasse. Note the European look of the city.

The buildings at the harbor of Tsingtau, China.

The transport ship Spreewald, Tsingtau, China.

The transport ship Rugia. The Spreewald and Rugia were the III. See-Bataillon's transport from Germany to China.

Manöver-Kritik. Critique and review of the maneuvers. Note the variety of uniforms and headgear.

NCOs in field garb and equipment stand apart on the right. Two are wearing "maneuver bands" on their tschakos.

More reviews. Note the officer with an uncovered pickelhaube, second from the left.

One Naval and two See-Bataillon officers pose with a high ranking Chinese in the center.

On the Firing Line. Enlisted men with Gew.98 rifles, Stg.98 bayonets, and full packs on maneuvers.

In Action. Note the highly elevated rear sight on the Gew.98 held by the man second from the left.

On the Firing Line. A good view of Imperial Marines and their equipment.

A Rest. Note the tschakos are being worn without their field covers. Rifles are stacked in the background.

Around the Field Kitchen. One man wears a visorless feldmütze; the others are in 1908 "Dienstmütze mitshirm" with a single national kokarde.

Chopping firewood for the field kitchen. All but two men are wearing blue Litewkas; the others in grey six button tunics.

Marines at the venerable K.P. duty of peeling potatoes.

Enjoying the Noonday Meal.

Before the Action. Field covers on the tschakos, full packs, blue Litewkas mixed with grey tunics, and Gew.98s are in the order of the day.

In a Rocky Valley near Lauschau. Rough terrain at best.

Another view of the Lauschau Valley.

In the Field. Note the kneeling man chopping firewood.

A cool day in the field. 1909. Note the use of the dark blue mantels, coupled with a man in a tropical helmet in the center.

The same group without mantels pose before their connected shelterhalfs, or zeltbahns

An interesting view of zeltbahns in the foreground laced together forming one long tent. 1909.

II Kompagnie III. See Batl. Company outing.

Another view of the II Kompagnie outing.

Manöver, 1909. Wagener's machine gun unit was equipped with the Maxim MG01, the forerunner of the lighter weight MG08.

An excellent view of the MG01 and crew in a firing position. Note the extended legs of the sled mount. 1909.

An officer with binoculars directs the field of fire of his MG01 crew. Manöver. 1909.

The terraced terrain of coastal China is evident in this photograph. Several MG01 crews can be seen. Manöver, 1909.

A rest pause after engagement. Interesting to note all horses are saddled and some have carbine boots slung for the Kar.88s.

Maschinengewehr aus dem Marsch. A team of horses pulls a two-wheeled cart, a schlitten 01, loaded with an MG01 and accessories. Note the two men working the brakes while on the steep downgrade.

Artillerie in Stellung. An FK96 in position, while other guns can be seen in the background of an unusually level area.

Wagener's "Korporalschaft", or unit, on a company outing.

Another view of Wagener's unit. Note the second man from the left is armed with a three-barreled "Drilling" civilian hunting gun.

Rest break during the company outing. A Chinese accompanies the group, sitting on the left.

Auf Polizeistation Marines in unusual turned-up wide-brimmed hats and visored caps pose with an accordion player.

Marines and Mandarins. Tsingtau, 1909.

Ein Sonntagnachmittag. No work, no duty, Sunday afternoon.

The best unit in the company shooting match gets their reward. Note the interesting tap arrangement on the beer keg in the center.

The caption reads Auf Polizeistation and interestingly shows the unusual wide-brimmed hats being worn in various ways. No reference has yet been found regarding this style of headgear.

Three Football Players is the caption for this photograph.

L/R: Zimmermann, Wech, and Wagener, the album owner, enjoy a Sunday afternoon beer in an outdoor setting.

A German family pose near their quarters at Kiautschou.

A gate through a Chinese protective city wall.

A parade being held in honor of the Kaiser's 50th birthday, January 1909.

The mole, Tsingtau Harbor.

The Imperial German Naval "Torpedoboot S90". The S90 was of a Thornycraft design, 400 tons and built in 1898, one of twelve of the type.

The German East Asiatic fleet underway near Tsingtau.

View of the defensive fort, Tsingtau.

Fieldmarshal Apell conducts an inspection of the troops.

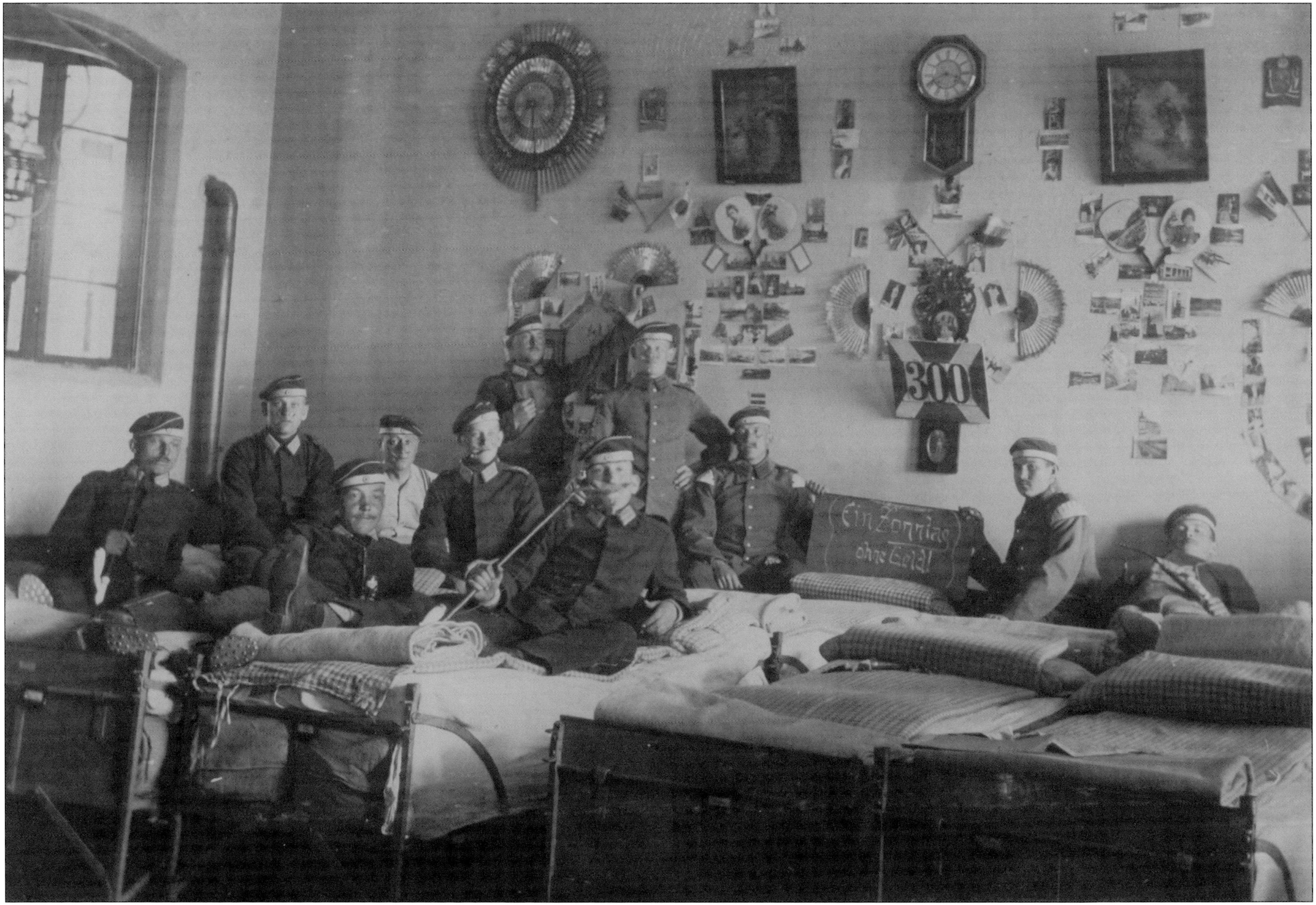

Stube 42, Room 42, which well may have been where Wagener lived. Close inspection of the wall decoration reveals oriental fans, postcards, photographs, miniature flags, and wall clock reading about 8:15.

Employment or personal duty hour. Over the beds is folded mosquito netting. The sign being held, "Parole Heimatt", literally translates 'password home'.

An evening snack being enjoyed in a barracks room.

Tsingtau Harbor.

Tsingtau from a different angle.

The channel out to sea from the Tsingtau Harbor.

The outer roadstead from Tsingtau.

An oil fire rages in Tsingtau Harbor.